JAZZ
A to Z

A guide to the originators and innovators and their best recordings

David Clune

Illustrations by Kevin O'Donnell

Connor Court Publishing

CONTENTS

ACKNOWLEDGMENTS

It was thanks to Rodney Cavalier that these articles were originally published in the *Southern Highlands Newsletter*. His backing and encouragement were essential. Milton Cockburn provided professional editorial advice, plus a good line: "To be a great jazz musician do you have to have a nickname and a substance abuse problem?" Tony Baldwin was generous with his encyclopaedic knowledge of jazz history. John Gourlay introduced me to much great jazz and provided feedback on many of the original drafts. Bob Irwin was a constant source of encouragement. I am greatly indebted to Kevin O'Donnell for his excellent illustrations which bring the text to life. I owe a debt to Anthony Cappello at Connor Court for taking on the project and seeing it through to publication with his usual professionalism. Also at Connor Court, Michael Gilchrist, who has a passion for and knowledge of jazz equalling my own, ensured a quality publication. Finally, my greatest debt is to my wife Ros and my musician daughter Meg who were, as always, my strongest supporters – and patiently listened to a lot of jazz.

David Clune

AUTHOR BIOGRAPHY

Dr David Clune OAM was for many years the Manager of the NSW Parliament's Research Service and the Parliament's Historian. He is currently an Honorary Associate in the Department of Government and International Relations at the University of Sydney. After writing extensively about Australian politics and history, he has now returned to his first love, jazz.

INTRODUCTION

When I was growing up in Sydney in the 1950s and 60s we had no gramophone at home. The only music my parents listened to on the wireless was classical. One day, taking a break from my final year high school studies, I tuned my transistor – remember them? – to a pop station. I was hooked, especially when I heard the Beatles, the Rolling Stones and Simon and Garfunkel. Soon after, I went through another evolution in listening taste. I heard Eric Clapton, Jimmy Page, Jeff Beck, Jimi Hendrix, Duane Allman. Someone had written "Clapton is God" backstage of the school hall much to the disgust of the Christian Brothers. But I had this constant niggle: how come these guys can play such brilliant solos yet so many rock groups whose LPs I spend my hard-earned dollars on are so disappointing? Enter jazz.

At Sydney University in the 1970s – in the halcyon days of self-liberation, self-expansion and, in some cases, self-destruction – I met guys who were into jazz. They told me Miles Davis was cool when they were at high school. I couldn't believe it – he played a trumpet! They also introduced me to the ABC's jazz programs: Eric Child, who was more on the swinging side, and Arch McKirdy with his oh so cool *Music to Midnight* – he was once sent up as "Arn Chacumfy". This was a revolution. It was complex stuff to listen to: few vocals and long solos. But amazingly consistent – these folks just played chorus after chorus and it was great.

Fast forward and I have spent a lifetime listening to and reading about jazz. It's been my consolation in times of trouble – the one true religion I'm tempted to say. In retirement, I had thought for some time of writing about my jazz journey. I approached Rodney Cavalier – to whose *Southern Highlands Newsletter* I have been a long-time subscriber and occasional contributor – to see if he was interested. Rodney was enthusiastic and I started at the beginning of 2017 to write my personal guide to jazz musicians from A to Z. Six years later I completed the series, a total of 31 articles about 47 musicians. A number of people were kind enough to suggest that I should publish the series in full. This book is the result. The text has been extensively revised and expanded for publication.

I have written about those whose music I find special and consider to be great jazz musicians – the originators and innovators. I have to stress that it is a selective and personal overview – the two things on the side of your head are really the best guide to what you enjoy in music. Many famous names are included, some omitted, and I have added a few obscure ones whose work, I think, rates with the greats. Occasionally, I express an opinion that is heretical according to conventional critical dogma.

In the entries, I attempt to give an account of the musician's life (often tragic), their style, significance, best recordings, the type of jazz they played, and some musicological context. Musicians I decided didn't necessitate an individual entry (sometimes a tough call) are often discussed in a related entry, for example, Chet Baker under Gerry Mulligan.

The styles I have covered include New Orleans, swing, bebop, hard bop, west coast cool and free bop. I must confess that I find the "new thing" of the 1960s unlistenable – my limitation, if you will. So, you will find no mention in these pages of Ornette Coleman, Eric Dolphy, Cecil Taylor and their like. As my dear old aunt used to tell me: if you can't say anything nice about someone, say nothing.

I hope this book will be of value to the novice and of interest to aficionados – and that those who read it have as much fun as I did writing it.

David Clune July 2023

1. LOUIS ARMSTRONG (1901-71)

"A" is absolutely, awesomely, amazingly for Armstrong. To me, four jazz soloists are uniquely compelling – even Eskimos in an igloo would be entranced on first hearing: Louis, Sidney Bechet, Charlie Parker and John Coltrane.

Louis Daniel Armstrong was born on 4 August 1901 in the wildest part of a wild town: a district in New Orleans so disorderly it was known as "the battlefield". His father abandoned the family soon after Louis was born, his mother worked occasionally as a prostitute, and young Louis roamed the streets. What lifted him out of the squalor, vice and violence was precocious virtuosity on the cornet. From an early age Armstrong was working professionally. His fame grew exponentially and he played with major band leaders like Joe "King" Oliver and Fletcher Henderson.

The Okeh label, a major producer of records aimed at black consumers, decided Armstrong was a good proposition. On 12 November 1925 Louis entered the studio with a pickup band he called the Hot Five (it later expanded to Hot Seven) and cut his first sides as a leader. Now I'm going to commit heresy: I don't particularly like the 1925 and 1926 recordings. The band is still a traditional New Orleans unit, with the front line improvising collectively. Louis was starting to invent the jazz soloist, and he often blazes out of the ensemble, notably on "Cornet Chop Suey". Of the rest, only Johnny Dodds on clarinet has claims to being a serious improviser. Trombonist "Kid" Ory was an inconsistent player. The band jolts along like a Model T Ford on a rough road. Particularly inappropriate are the clunking piano chords of Lil Hardin – still, she was attractive, light-skinned, educated and, as such, an asset to Louis as his (second) wife.

I have to admit that Miss Lil did rise to the occasion in a most unlikely situation. In 1930 she and Louis recorded "Blue Yodel No. 9" with Jimmie Rodgers, "the Singing Brakeman". It was a pretty ordinary song: "Along come a police he took me by the arm. It was down in Memphis on the corner of Beale and Main. He says big boy you'll have to tell me your name. I said you'll find my name on the tail of my shirt". Somehow, the emotional depth of Louis' bluesy accompaniment turns it into a memorable performance.

Another problem was that some of the early material Okeh wanted Armstrong to record was awful, for example, "He Likes it Slow" with the comedy duo of Butterbeans and Susie and "The King of the Zulus at a Chitlin' Rag" – ouch! He was reduced to playing tin whistle on one track. I also find May Alix's shrill vocals distracting from some fine Armstrong playing on numbers like "Big Butter and Egg Man". Louis didn't care as long as he got paid. In one of the classic miscalculations of all time, he opted for $50 per session rather than royalties so he could go out and party.

Things evolved rapidly. By 1927 Louis is the undoubted star, dragging the band along behind him. There are still lots of moments when I drum my fingers waiting for him to start soloing – but is it worth the wait! On tracks like "Twelfth Street Rag", "Melancholy Blues", "Hotter Than That" and "Wild Man Blues" Armstrong's solos are magnificent – as good as any jazz that has ever been recorded. Another recording from that year, "Potato Head Blues", was made famous by Woody Allen in the 1979 movie Manhattan when his screen character said it was one of the things that made life worth living.

From 1928, when he abandoned the cornet for trumpet, Louis reached a new level of brilliance. It was not only technical, though that was unparalleled: when he first played in London a delegation of local trumpeters insisted on inspecting his instrument backstage as they were convinced it contained some cunning device to allow him to achieve what seemed impossible. Armstrong had an incredible range but, unlike other well-known trumpeters, never screamed when he played high. His sense of timing and structure were impeccable. Louis also had a superb tone, not only penetratingly clear but rich and warm. Above all, no matter how many high Cs, Fs and Gs he hit, his playing was always musical – never of the "hard to do and hard to listen to variety".

Earl "Fatha" Hines was a virtuoso, innovator and major influence on future pianists. As well as having a strong left hand, Hines played long melodic lines with his right, a development that would reach its apotheosis with "Bud" Powell in the 1950s. Earl and Louis met playing pool at the back of the black musicians' union hall in Chicago and soon became friends. Hines joined the Hot Five in 1928. He added thoughtful, at times almost classical, solos as a foil to Louis' fireworks. Hines composed an enduring standard, "A Monday Date". It begins with some typically lively dialogue:

> Armstrong: Hey, hey Earl Hines, why don't you let us in on some of that good music, pops?
>
> Hines: Well, let's get together then.
>
> Armstrong: Well, all right. C'mon tune up boys. How's that sound?
>
> Hines: Sounds pretty good.
>
> Armstrong: Yeah, that sounds pretty good – bet you wouldn't say that if you had half a pint of Mrs Searcy's gin! Well, we're going to play anyway. (To Zutty Singleton) C'mon, Zulu, whip them cymbals.

The partnership reached a peak with the duet "Weather Bird". Other classics (it's hard to choose) are "Save It Pretty Mama", "St James Infirmary", "Tight like This" and "West End Blues". It has said of the last of these:

> It begins with an unaccompanied clarion cadenza, twelve seconds of bravura playing so dazzling that no other trumpeter has ever quite succeeded in replicating it … Earl Hines adds an elegantly flowing piano chorus before Armstrong takes up his trumpet again and breaks into one of his most magisterial solos, beginning with a single note held without discernible effort for four measures, as if time meant nothing to him, and then plunging into the heart of the blues (Ken Burns and Geoffrey Ward, *Jazz: a history of America's music*, Pimlico, 2001).

Armstrong was maturing at an incredible rate. By 1929, his playing had a mellow, serene beauty. Although the brilliance was un-dimmed, it was displayed more sparingly. The tempos were often slower and Louis tended to stay closer to the melody. This new style was complemented by his vocals which were increasingly promi-nent. Armstrong expert Brian Peerless has noted that Louis' sing-ing had its own distinctive influence: "His ability to reshape lyrics, giving them a new dimension and depth of meaning the composer could never have hoped for, is unique".

Louis was plundering other bands for good sidemen, most no-tably "Red" Allen, JC Higginbotham and Albert Nicholas from Fletcher Henderson. "I Can't Give You Anything but Love", "When You're Smiling", "Some of These Days" and "Black and Blue" are transcendent tracks. My personal favourite from this period is "St Louis Blues". Over four carefully constructed choruses Armstrong builds to a climax as stunning as Ravel's "Bolero".

In the early 1930s, Louis fronted a big band organised by trum-peter Zilner Randolph. It has traditionally come in for a hammer-ing from the critics, and there is some truth in the charge that the cats lived hard and played loose, but the band suited Armstrong and it swung (unevenly at times). Jazz scholar Dan Morgenstern has summed the situation up:

> It makes no sense to judge an Armstrong big band by the same standards as are used for Ellington, Basie or Goodman. It is not intended to be a self-sufficient creative unit; it is essen-tially there to back a virtuoso instrumentalist and singer who in a very real sense is the whole show … Louis always made sure he had a good rhythm section, anchored by a strong sup-portive drummer.

Morgenstern adds: "You can hear him practically will his sometimes less than ideal supporting cast into the tempos and grooves he wants". The masterpieces continued to flow (although not as consistently): "Sweethearts on Parade", "The Peanut Vendor", "Blue Again", "When Your Lover Has Gone", "I've Got the World on a String", "I've Got a Right to Sing the Blues", "When It's Sleepy Time Down South" (for a long time Louis' theme song).

Armstrong took yet another change of direction in the 1940s. Big bands were becoming increasingly expensive and unfashionable and Louis returned to performing with small groups. In May 1946, he put down three superb tracks with his Dixieland Seven. A personal favourite is "Where the Blues were Born in New Orleans". After a bantering opening in which Louis calls off the band, he tears into a smoking hot rideout. If you don't tap your foot to this, see a doctor as you may be dead!

Trombonist Jack Teagarden soon became a regular associate. Personally and musically, it was a compatible partnership. Although Teagarden was a gifted soloist with a very individual vocal style, he never tried to steal the show from the boss. He happily hammed it up with Louis in routines like "Rockin' Chair". In May 1947 Armstrong gave a concert at New York Town Hall with a small group. The program consisted of standards and old favourites played with a new vigour and freshness, to the delight of the audience and critics. It was the end of the big band.

For the rest of his career Louis performed with a sextet known as the All Stars. The difficulty of the transition should not be underestimated. According to Morgenstern: "To switch from being featured in front of a big band to being the lead instrumental voice in a small group was a monumental task that only trumpeters over the age of 46 can fully understand, but Pops pulled it off in Herculean style".

A fine example of the All Stars at their peak is a concert at Symphony Hall in Boston in November 1947. It really was an all-star band, featuring Teagarden, former "Duke" Ellington clarinettist Barney Bigard, and "Big Sid" Catlett on drums. "Big T", in particular, never played or sang better than on his feature, "Stars Fell on Alabama".

For Louis, the All Stars was like an Australian politician becoming High Commissioner in London: a comfortable and undemanding end to a notable career. For the rest of his life he toured to increasing acclaim with the same format, same songs, same predictable hokum – and occasional reminders of the trumpet glories of the past. Wynton Marsalis has remarked on "the level of soul and perfectly refined tone colour" of the later Armstrong.

Louis became a post-war institution with his toothy "satchel mouth" grin (the source of his nickname "Satchmo"), throaty chuckle, carefree manner and amiable personality. He was safe and amusing compared to other jazz musicians who became aggressively involved in the civil rights struggle. Basically, it seems that the reality wasn't too different. Louis was always the happy-go-lucky abandoned kid that made good beyond his wildest dreams: owning a place with an indoor bathroom and meeting the Pope (in fact, two of them) were proud boasts.

Some jazz critics and scholars have written learned articles about Louis not understanding the difference between being an entertainer and a musician – the so-called dichotomy of the performing artist – hence recording a lot of questionable music. He was even accused of "Uncle Tomism" for recording songs about "picaninnies" and "curly headed babies". What a load of codswallop! Unlike some academics, Louis never had the luxury of a guaranteed meal ticket. His life was spent, as the title of one of his recordings goes, "Hustlin' and Bustlin' for Baby" (there were quite a number). Who at the time in their wildest dreams ever thought that jazz would come to be regarded as an art form or "America's classical music"? Although there are some shockers like "Laughin' Louie" and "She's the Daughter of a Planter From Havana", the artistic quality of Armstrong's achievement is, in fact, extraordinarily high. As Morgenstern says, "the rhapsodic trumpet work, of course, is beyond the realm of political correctness".

Throughout his career Louis recorded masterpiece after masterpiece and showed no sign of standing still creatively. Very few other jazz musicians could make such a claim. He died of a heart attack on 6 July 1971.

2. "COUNT" BASIE (1904-84)

William James Basie was born on 21 August 1904 in Red Bank, New Jersey. Leaving school at the age of 14, he played piano in silent movie theatres for a living. Basie haunted Harlem listening to the stride masters such as James P Johnson and "Fats" Waller. He soon began touring extensively on the vaudeville circuit. One of the acts Basie was with went broke in Kansas City in 1927 and he was stuck there. It proved to be the making of him. The town had a vibrant jazz scene in the dives and clubs and a unique stomping blues style. The most famous local band was that of Benny Moten which

Basie joined. When Moten died in 1935, Basie formed his own outfit. Aware of "King" Oliver and "Duke" Ellington, Basie created a peerage for himself and adopted the style "Count" – it stuck for the rest of his life.

I'm no fan of big bands featuring mechanical playing and brazen blaring. There is a tension between jazz as an art of improvisation and bands playing tight arrangements. Basie solved this by having a lithe, driving rhythm section as an underpinning and leaving lots of space for his soloists. There were few written arrangements – they usually developed spontaneously from interaction between the Count and his colleagues. The Basie band combined the punch of a big ensemble with the freedom of a small group.

Bassist Walter Page, drummer Jo Jones and guitarist Freddie Green were with Basie for most of his career. They have been described as the greatest rhythm section in the history of jazz – though Wyn Kelly, Paul Chambers and "Philly" Joe Jones might have a say on that one. Page's advice to his colleagues was to lower the volume and increase the intensity.

Then there is the Count's piano playing. By the mid-1930s he had moved on from "the steady, four beats to the bar left hand that the masters of Harlem stride had taught him in favour of spare, witty fills and asides that commented on the music being played and spurred his men to greater effort. Even a single note, Count Basie said, can swing" (Ken Burns and Geoffrey Ward, *Jazz: a history of America's music*, Pimlico, 2001). In his solos, the silences are as important as the notes, like space on the wall around a great painting.

Basie's band included an array of talented soloists, most notably tenor player Lester Young, one of the most influential saxophonists jazz has produced. Young's light, sinuous playing was revolutionary. Herschel Evans was the other Basie tenor. He was of the Coleman Hawkins school, with a more robust tone. The Count used the contrast between them to good effect. After Evans' untimely death, "Chu" Berry then "Buddy" Tate took over the role. The stalwarts of the brass section were trumpeters "Buck" Clayton and Harry "Sweets" Edison, and Benny Morton and Dickie Wells on trombone. Jimmy Rushing's bluesy vocals were an added attraction – because of his girth and height he was known as "Mr Five by Five".

In 1936, jazz promoter and critic (and Benny Goodman's brother-in-law) John Hammond heard the Basie band, declared it the best in the US, and arranged for the Count to come to New York. The band sounded raw and rudimentary compared to sophisticated outfits like Ellington's, but it had a propulsive swing that blew the town apart. There are few more exciting sounds in jazz than the early Basie band in full cry.

Dave Kapp of Decca persuaded the Count to sign a recording contract with him. It has long been received wisdom that Basie was tricked into a punitive arrangement before Hammond could sign him for the label he worked for, Columbia. Jazz pianist, critic and historian Tony Baldwin questions this:

> In hindsight, Dave Kapp's terms may not seem very generous, but they were no worse than what any other largely unknown, provincial black band could have expected at the time. This was still very much the Depression, and Kapp was taking a considerable risk by signing Basie at all. We really only have the self-aggrandising Hammond's word that his own terms would have been any better, or indeed that, as a freelance with no particular executive status within ARC/Columbia, he would have even had the leverage to contract this then ob-

scure outfit. While the Count's three years with Decca obviously didn't make him much money, Decca's superb technical standards certainly helped to seal his reputation (email to the author).

The 1937-39 Decca recordings are the best Basie made. Among the classics are "Pennies from Heaven", "One O'clock Jump", "Topsy", "Every Tub", "Jumpin' at the Woodside". By the time Basie finally signed with Columbia the early spontaneity was fading, though there were still some fine performances, such as "Miss Thing", "Pound Cake", "Tickle Toe", and "9.20 Special" (featuring Coleman Hawkins).

The studio can have a constricting effect on jazz musicians and the technological limitations of the recording process in the 1930s meant performances were limited to three minutes, often not enough time to really loosen up. Fortunately, a number of live recordings of the Basie band in its prime were made from radio broadcasts. In 2003, Sony issued a Basie compilation, *America's Number One Band*, which includes a disc of adrenalin-pumping performances from the Savoy Ballroom, the Famous Door and other regular Basie venues, many never previously released. A personal favourite is "They Can't Take that Away from Me" featuring Billie Holiday at her finest.

There are also some memorable small group recordings from the 1930s and 40s. The session in 1936 that marked the debut of Lester Young has been described by celebrated jazz producer Orrin Keepnews as "legendary, pioneering and almost mystical". In 1942, Basie recorded eight tracks featuring Buck Clayton and Don Byas (who briefly replaced Young), released as *Blues by Basie*. Particularly enjoyable is the mellow "after hours" feel of "How Long Blues", "Sugar Blues", and "St Louis Blues".

In the 1950s, Basie formed his "New Testament" band. It had a predominantly arranged sound, featuring more ensemble and less solo work. He had a hit album in 1958 with *The Atomic Mr Basie*. It has been praised by the critics but (heresy warning!) I find it loud, formulaic and devoid of the freshness of the "Old Testament" recordings. The later Basie band was known as the "swing machine", but the latter predominated over the former.

In his final years, Basie returned to working with small groups. The results are best described as mixed. There was, however, a stand-out session in 1975 with tenor player "Zoot" Sims, a Lester Young disciple and an ideal partner. As annotator Benny Green says, the Count displays throughout "a manifestation of creative energy which is amazing" and "still swings like the clappers".

Basie continued to tour and record into the 1980s. He died of pancreatic cancer on 26 April 1984.

3. SIDNEY BECHET (1897-1959)

Sidney Bechet was born in New Orleans on 14 May 1897 into a middle class Creole family. He had taught himself to play clarinet by the age of six and as a teenager worked with many local bands. Later he took up the difficult soprano saxophone and created a unique sound featuring a truly feral vibrato. Bechet was a brilliant soloist, as innovative as Armstrong (with whom he recorded), but unlike Louis he was not a pleasant person. Temperamental, wilful, egotistical are words that come to mind. Bechet was convicted of assaulting a woman in London in 1920 and deported. In 1928, he shot it out in a Parisian street with a colleague who had criticised his playing. Bechet wounded a number of innocent by-standers and spent 11 months in a French gaol. Sidney's difficult personality hampered his career and prevented him from achieving the fame of Armstrong, although jazz fans – like me – forget all the unpleasantness when they listen to his solos.

"Duke" Ellington regarded Bechet as "the symbol of jazz" and "the greatest of all the originators". British music critic Max Harrison has said that Bechet's playing conveys "a passion, almost an ecstasy, that very few jazz masters have paralleled and which aptly mirrors his dominating personality and restless wandering life" (M Harrison, C Fox and E Thacker, *The Essential Jazz Records: ragtime to swing*, Da Capo, 1988).

Bechet's regular outfit was a small group, the aptly named New Orleans Feetwarmers, usually featuring trumpeter Tommy Ladnier as the other horn. Sidney's specialty was soaring above the ensemble, bringing numbers to a thrilling conclusion. He dominated almost every band he played in. Exhilarating early Bechet performances are "Maple Leaf Rag", "Really the Blues" and "When You and I Were Young Maggie".

When times got tough in the Depression, Bechet and Ladnier opened a shop in Harlem – the former ironed shirts and the latter shined shoes – and lived upstairs. In the evenings Bechet cooked up a mess of gumbo (apparently, it was as dangerous to question his culinary skills as his musical ones) and they jammed with friends.

A refugee from Hitler's Germany, Alfred Lion, arrived In New York in 1936 and soon after established Blue Note records. Although the label is usually associated with bebop and beyond, it initially focussed on the 1940s traditional jazz revival. One of Lion's favourites was Bechet whom he recorded many times, often in the company of other New Orleans veterans such as trumpeters "Bunk" Johnson and Sidney De Paris, and clarinettist Albert Nicholas. The Blue Notes re-established Bechet's reputation. As well as the hot, stomping sides, there were some magical slower performances. An emotionally charged "Summertime" on soprano became a hit. Even better is "Blue Horizon". Critic Dan Morgenstern has described it as Bechet's "clarinet masterpiece and, beyond that, simply one of the greatest blues ever put on record. It's Sidney all the way, building through six choruses of 12 bar blues with remarkable beauty and logic".

In 1951, Bechet moved permanently to France. He spent the last eight years of his life there, performing, recording and being increasingly lionised as a celebrity – a park in Antibes was named Sidney Bechet Square. A notable record from this period, with French pianist Martial Solal, is *When a Soprano Meets a Piano*, recorded in 1957. Bechet died in Paris of lung cancer on 14 May 1959.

4. "BIX" BEIDERBECKE (1903-31)

Leon Bismark (sic) Beiderbecke was born on 10 March 1903 in Davenport, Iowa, the son of a prosperous coal and timber merchant. A child prodigy on piano, Bix was seduced by jazz and taught himself to play cornet. By 1922, he was working professionally. Tragically, young Bismark proved to be no man of iron where liquor was involved. Alcoholism hampered his career and lead to his death at the age of 28.

Armstrong, Bechet and Beiderbecke are the holy trinity of soloists in the formative years of jazz. But Bix was different: his playing was cool yet he swung; although he was technically gifted, there were few pyrotechnics. Bix danced lightly above the rhythm. His solos are lean, carefully constructed intellectual creations that never go in a predictable direction but end up sounding just right. Bix's singing tone has a purity like the sound that results from flicking the side of a Waterford crystal glass. Critic Dan Morgenstern has referred to his "cornet poetry".

Many of Bix's records were marred by poor sound quality, corny vocals or inappropriate ensembles, such as Paul Whiteman's ponderous orchestra. His greatest music was recorded in 1927 with his friend Frankie "Tram" Trumbauer. Tram, who played C melody sax which has a lighter sound than the more familiar tenor instrument, had a personal and musical rapport with Bix and managed to keep him on the wagon – some of the time. These small group sessions featured the cream of New York jazz musicians: Eddie Lang, Joe Venuti, Adrian Rollini, Jimmy Dorsey, "Pee Wee" Russell. It was the birth of chamber jazz. Although the standard is consistently high, stand-out tracks are "Singin' the Blues", "I'm Coming Virginia", "Riverboat Shuffle", and "Way Down Yonder in New Orleans".

Beiderbecke had ambitions as a composer. He enjoyed the music of Debussy and Ravel and aspired to incorporate their style into jazz. In 1927 Bix recorded a solo piano composition, "In a Mist". Three other Beiderbecke piano pieces, "Flashes", "In the Dark", and "Candlelights", were given their first recordings by Jess Stacy in the 1930s. They are intriguing, impressionistic compositions. In his 1993 Maybeck Hall recital, Ralph Sutton played "In a Mist" and "In the Dark", giving some idea of their potentialities.

In June 1930, Bix, Benny Goodman and Jack Teagarden recorded a session under the leadership of Irving Mills, later "Duke" Ellington's manager. Beiderbecke was in bad physical shape, but his solo on "Loved One" explodes out of the ensemble like a supernova. It was his last great performance. Bix died of pneumonia on 6 August 1931.

5. ART BLAKEY (1919-90)

In the 1940s a new style of jazz emerged known as bebop or simply bop. Mainly associated with Charlie Parker, John Birks "Dizzy" Gillespie and Earl "Bud" Powell, it became fashionable with the young and hip. Bop reinvented the role of the drummer. Previously, the man on the traps was restricted to keeping time with the occasional solo break, hence the old joke about a big band consisting of a dozen musicians and a drummer. Bop percussionists were central to the music, driving and challenging the horn men in the front line. Instead of continually keeping a steady pulse, the bop drummer "dropped bombs" behind soloists. British jazz broadcaster Mark White has noted that the boppers

> rearranged the internal balance of the rhythm section so that the bass player became the only man who laid down a constant beat. The drummer confined his basic rhythm to the use of his hi-hat cymbals (sometimes not even that), using the rest of his kit for accents, breaks and explosions, notably with the bass drum.

Influential bop drummers were Kenny Clarke, Elvin Jones, Max Roach, and Art Blakey. In my opinion, the last was the greatest of them all. As well as being a virtuoso, Art was a musical drummer – his solos were exhilarating but never descended into mindless thrashing. I have to say that I am of the heretical opinion that audiences often applaud loudly at the end of a drum solo because they are so damn glad it's over. Never with Blakey. He was also a gifted band leader. Blakey composed "from the drum stool, shaping the course of each improvisation by way of the complexity or otherwise of his own contributions, now driving the soloist on to extra vehemence with a battery of accents and cross-rhythms, now letting him set his own emotional pace with a quietly swinging background beat" (Michael James in M Harrison, A Morgan, R Atkins, M James, J Cooke eds, *Modern Jazz, 1945-70: the essential records*, Aquarius Books, 1975).

Arthur Blakey was born on 11 October 1919 in Pittsburgh. He learnt piano from an early age but switched to drums as a teenager. Blakey had a sadly typical jazz life. His single mother died soon after childbirth and he was fostered out. He dropped out of school early for the restless, insecure life of a jazz musician. He was beaten so badly by a white policeman that he needed major skull surgery. Heroin addiction was a continuing problem.

By the 1950s, Art was regularly backing many of the bop giants. Jazz had separated into two streams: on the west coast it was laid-back and cool, in New York it became hard bop. The essence of hard bop was the beat and the blues – tough, driving music with often unmemorable melodies and little in the way of arrangements. Soloists were the core, one blowing after the other. Fortunately, jazz at this stage was producing an amazing succession of gifted players to feed the flame.

The quintessential hard bop band was Blakey's Jazz Messengers. It had its genesis in a sparkling live set recorded in 1954 at the famous jazz club Birdland, issued under the name of the Art Blakey Quintet. The band featured pianist Horace Silver, altoist Lou Donaldson and Clifford Brown on trumpet. "Brownie" was the new trumpet star. His technical mastery, improvisational skill and lustrous tone are displayed to the full on *A Night at Birdland*. Tragically, he died in a car accident two years later.

Blakey and Silver established the Jazz Messengers as a co-operative and in 1955 released an album under the latter's name with an all-star band: trumpeter Kenny Dorham, tenor sax player Hank Mobley and bassist Doug Watkins. It was a potent example of pristine hard bop. Silver, an under-rated composer, wrote all the numbers. His penchant for gospel is evident on *The Preacher* which became a hit and jazz standard. After this, Blakey and Silver went their own ways. Horace was a percussive, rhythmic player, well suited to bop, although he also had a more reflective side. For the rest of his career he led a series of superior small groups and produced consistently rewarding records. Most famous is *Song for my Father* from 1965 (rock group Steely Dan stole a riff from the title track for their hit "Rikki Don't Lose That Number"). In 1996, Horace released a record aptly named *Hard Bop Grandpop*.

In 1956, Blakey formed what for me is the definitive version of the Jazz Messengers. The star soloist was Jackie McLean on alto sax. Jackie's scintillating style and primal tone were well suited to Blakey's concept. He hunches in behind and drives McLean relentlessly. Trumpeter Bill Hardman was a more restrained but resourceful player. This band made a classic recording in 1956 simply named *Hard Bop* – what more is there to say except listen?

McLean soon left and was replaced by another stimulating soloist, tenor player Johnny Griffin, "the Little Giant" (if you want to hear some breath-taking sax check out his 1956 debut on Blue Note). This band made a celebrated 1958 recording with Thelonius Monk. Jazz producers, especially Norman Granz, have always loved these meetings of titans – the logic seemed to be that two big names equalled double the profit. More often than not it didn't work but this one brought out the best in both Blakey and Monk.

Throughout his career, Blakey reinvigorated the Messengers by hiring the cream of young musicians. As well as fresh input, it provided an unparalleled education for the new generation. According to Art: "Why should I try to keep the young fellows with me? Let them grow and get out and form more good jazz groups. Besides there are other young players waiting for their big chance to be heard". It was, however, tough love: "I'm always kicking them in the ass. It's as much as anyone can do to keep up with me".

In 1960, trumpeter Lee Morgan and tenor player Wayne Shorter were the Messengers' new front line. Both were major talents, and Shorter a gifted composer. Shorter and Morgan were influenced by the modal jazz pioneered by Miles Davis on *Kind of Blue* and Shorter would soon become a member of Miles' great "free bop" quintet. It was a different, more sophisticated version of the Messengers. This band's best known disc is *A Night in Tunisia*, which opens with a show-stopping version of the title tune. The rest of the album is quieter and more introspective.

The following year, Morgan was replaced by Freddie Hubbard, and trombonist Curtis Fuller joined the front line. Shorter was now the musical director and main composer. Hubbard's "feisty brightness and Fuller's sober quick-fire solos" served as "a memorable counterweight to Shorter's private, dark improvisations" (*Penguin Guide to Jazz*, 6th ed). More great records followed, including *Mosaic* and *Buhaina's Delight*.

While many jazz musicians, including Shorter, moved into fusion in the 1970s and made a fortune, Art remained true to the faith. Blakey told a story about meeting one of his former employees, trumpeter Donald Byrd, who had crossed over into soul and had a million-selling hit record: "I looked at Donald and he had a lot of money, but he had this big potbelly and he looked stressed and he didn't look healthy and I said, 'Donald, I never saw an armoured car following a hearse.'"

Blakey led the Messengers for 35 years, "the living, laughing symbol of the music's extraordinary resilience. Even when growing deafness made it hard for him to hear his soloists, he continued to outswing musicians half his age" (Ken Burns and Geoffrey Ward, *Jazz: a history of America's music*, Pimlico, 2001). A heavy smoker, Art Blakey died of lung cancer on 16 October 1990.

6. RUBY BRAFF (1927-2003)

Reuben Braff was born in Boston on 16 March 1927. A self-taught cornetist, Ruby took an entirely different direction to other musicians of his generation – his main influence was Louis Armstrong rather than "Dizzy" Gillespie. Ruby's style matured into his own brand of mellow mainstream. The cornet helped create a rich, sonorous tone. He could still wail but at other times his playing was soft, lyrical and pensive. In his obituary for Braff in *The Guardian*, John Fordham said:

> He was one of the finest practitioners of his instrument, gifted with a rare fertility of ideas and an unerring control of their direction and shape. The way he would skitter playfully around a melody, steady himself with spare, carefully poised sounds, brightly attack an improvisation as good as the original, hold shimmering long notes, or duck in and out of a different tune, was endlessly fascinating (13 February 2003).

Ruby's musical contrariness, plus a certain contrariness of personality (he was known to his colleagues as "Mr Hyde and Mr Hyde"), impeded his early career. When he had work it was with swing era revival groups. In 1956 he recorded, *Braff!*, with another outstanding throwback, pianist "Big Dave" McKenna. Ruby was joined on four tracks by Coleman Hawkins and Ellington trombonist Lawrence Brown and was in no way outclassed by such distinguished company. *Hi-Fi Salute to Bunny* from the following year, a tribute to Swing trumpeter "Bunny" Berrigan, is another fine mainstream album. A 2007 compilation, *Ruby Braff with Hank Jones: Complete Recordings*, contains an essential distillation of his late 1950s work, including some duets with Roy Eldridge

Braff always preferred to work with small forces. He had a legendary partnership with pianist Ellis Larkins. Classically trained, Larkins was a much-praised accompanist, particularly for his work with Ella Fitzgerald. An ideal foil for Ruby, they recorded a series of duets in 1955, which they reprised in 1972 on the aptly named *Grand Reunion*. In 1994, the elder statesmen came together again and recorded a tribute to Irving Berlin. The best of the sequence, it has the gentle glow of autumn light.

In 1973, Braff formed a group with guitarist George Barnes, bassist Michael Moore and rhythm guitarist Wayne Wright. Barnes was a gifted soloist and a musically compatible partner for Ruby. They had a similar predilection for the Swing era and subtlety. Until Braff's short fuse brought the partnership to an end in 1975, the quartet produced some of the finest small group jazz ever recorded.

It was only natural that Ruby would join forces with the young fogey of the saxophone, Scott Hamilton. Born in 1954, Hamilton looked back to Swing as his inspiration and played tenor as well as the old masters of the 1930s. In 1985, they made two records with Scott's band, *A First* and *A Sailboat in The Moonlight*. Even better is the 1991 Ruby Braff and His New England Songhounds date. Backed by a dream line up – Dave McKenna, guitarist Howard Alden, bassist Frank Tate and drummer Alan Dawson – Ruby and Scott produced some superb, sophisticated, swinging music.

In his later years, Braff acquired an international reputation – though not as great as it should have been – and was in demand for concerts and recordings. In 2002, Ruby toured the UK. John Fordham recalled that "he looked as if he wouldn't make it from one gig to the next. But the moment he lifted the cornet to his lips, all thoughts of frailty and mortality evaporated … Everything he played was an affirmation of life and hope". Braff died of emphysema, heart failure and glaucoma on 9 February 2003.

7. DAVE BRUBECK (1920-2012)

David Warren Brubeck was born in Concord, California on 6 December 1920. His mother, who was a talented classical pianist, gave him lessons as a child. However, when Dave went to College of the Pacific at Stockton, California, he enrolled in veterinary science, intending to become a rancher like his father. The lure of music proved too great and Brubeck moved across the campus to the conservatory. His scholastic achievement was mixed, as he could not sight read and some of the stuffier staff disapproved of his interest in jazz. More successful was his time at Mills College, after Army service in the Second World War. Brubeck studied under composer Darius Milhaud who inspired his life-long interest in classical forms.

Brubeck formed a quartet with Paul Desmond on alto sax and started playing the college circuit, an unusual move at the time. It was raw, exhilarating music that was instantly popular. A 1953 live recording, *Jazz at Oberlin*, captured the atmosphere well. Dave signed with Columbia the next year and two further vibrant concert recordings followed, *Jazz Goes to College* and *Jazz Goes to Junior College*.

By the late 1950s the classic quartet was in place. Dave found the ideal rhythm section in bassist Gene Wright and drummer Joe Morello. Partially blind from birth, Morello featured on the quartet's biggest hit, "Take Five" (written by Desmond). Desmond was one of the greatest altoists in modern jazz. Although influenced by bop, he had a pure, sensuous, floating sound. Paul described his music as "like a dry martini". He said that he aimed for "clarity, emotional communication on a not too obvious level, form in a chorus that doesn't hit you over the head but is there if you look for it, humour, and construction that sounds logical in an unexpected way".

Brubeck's playing had its *longueurs* but Desmond was never less than excellent. In the 1960s, he recorded under his own name with guitarist Jim Hall. Sony released a boxed set in 2011 containing remastered and expanded versions of the six LPs Desmond made for RCA. Listening to them is like luxuriating in a spa bath with, yes, a dry martini.

Although loosely identified with the west coast cool genre, Brubeck's music has its own individual sound. He experimented with polyrhythms and unusual time signatures. An obituary for Brubeck in *The Economist* observed that "his use of folk songs and hymns and blues and birdcalls, his little snatches of homage to George Gershwin or Aaron Copland, and the freight-train urging of his playing, gave his jazz a flavour less of smoky dives than of open skies and plains" (15 December 2012).

In 1959, *Time Out* was released. It had the lot: blues, ballads, experimentation, and old fashioned stomping. The album sold over a million copies and became Brubeck's most famous record. Other impressive recordings from this period are *Jazz Impressions of Japan* and *Jazz Impressions of New York*.

Brubeck's playing was controversial. He was derided as a bombastic, self-indulgent pounder, and there were occasions when there was an element of truth in this. In fact, Brubeck could be an elegant pianist, spinning long single note lines. However, he often climaxed his solos with repeated heavy chords. Sometimes it worked, generating huge excitement, and sometimes it didn't, for example, in the overrated 1963 Carnegie Hall concert.

The reflective side of Brubeck is very much on display in his solo outings. Good examples are *Brubeck Plays Brubeck* and *Dave Brubeck Plays and Plays*, recorded at Dave's home in 1956 and 1957 respectively. In later life, Brubeck returned to solo performance and made some excellent recordings. Recommended are *Just You, Just Me* (1994) and *One Alone* (2000).

Another example of Dave in light, lyrical mode is an album of duets he made with Desmond in 1975. I have a friend who is a jazz aficionado who has made no secret of his disdain for Brubeck at the keyboard. I played this record for him in a "blindfold" test. He immediately identified Desmond but said: "The pianist is good but I can't place him". Thinking I was giving it away, I said: "Who's the pianist most identified with Desmond?" He replied firmly: "It can't be Dave Brubeck".

Throughout his career, Dave recorded prolifically – one might even say undiscriminatingly – and toured relentlessly. Brubeck's interest in classical music led to the composition of oratorios and cantatas. Although he took his music seriously, Dave was never ashamed of being popular, and he was immensely so – in 1975 an asteroid was named after him. Like Louis Armstrong, Brubeck was the jazz musician non-jazz fans had heard of. And like Louis, he was basically a decent, down-to-earth guy. Dave was devoted to his wife Iola and family. At one stage, in what might unkindly be described as a travelling nepotism show, he toured with three of his sons.

Brubeck died of heart failure on 5 December 2012 at the age of 91 and was working right up to the end. *The Economist* obituary quoted earlier summed up the man and his music:

> Critics said he was too 'European', too college-focused, that his music couldn't be danced to and hadn't got swing; he pointed out the happy feet tapping at his concerts, and the number of records he sold. Above all they found it hard to believe that the most successful jazz in America was being played by a family man, a laid-back Californian, modest, gentle and open, who would happily have been a rancher all his days – except that he couldn't live without performing, because the rhythm of jazz, under all his extrapolation and exploration, was, he had discovered, the rhythm of his heart.

8. BENNY CARTER (1907-2003)

Benny Carter was one of the protean figures of early jazz: arranger, composer, bandleader and multi-instrumentalist. If a musician didn't turn up for a date it was never a problem as Benny simply played the instrument himself. Alto sax was his main horn – he had a bright, polished sound that is instantly recognisable. Carter easily managed the most challenging double in jazz, playing excellent trumpet as well. Louis Armstrong admired his work. Whatever the instrument, Benny could swing hard or solo with elegance and finesse.

Born on 8 August 1907, **Bennett Lester Carter** grew up in Harlem surrounded by jazz. A self-taught prodigy, he was playing professionally at 17. Benny served his apprenticeship with some of the top big bands of the day – Fletcher Henderson, "Chick" Webb and McKinney's Cotton Pickers – and in the early 1930s formed his own outfit. Carter's solos and innovative arrangements made an immediate impact.

In 1935, Carter was hired by the BBC as an arranger for its dance band and moved to Britain, where he spent three productive years. There was a thriving European jazz scene and Benny was soon jamming and recording with local groups. His most famous London record (and composition) is "When Lights Are Low". Vocalist Elizabeth Welch warbles a little, but it is a memorable melody.

On his return to the US, Carter put together another big band. The recordings it made are "full of examples of his compact expertise as an orchestrator; the marvellous way in which he balances the different band sections in combination, separation and interaction" (Eric Thacker in M Harrison, C Fox and E Thacker, *The Essential Jazz Records: ragtime to swing*, Da Capo, 1988). The standout recording from this period is "All of Me", with a perfectly crafted reed arrangement and a Carter clarinet solo that is the glistening cherry on the cake.

Benny also recorded with a small unit, the Chocolate Dandies. The collective personnel included a galaxy of talent: Coleman Hawkins, "Chu" Berry and Ben Webster on tenor; Max Kaminsky, Roy Eldridge and Buck Clayton on trumpet. The 1940 and 1946 sessions, in particular, are vintage small group jazz, with superb solos and sympathetic interplay.

In the 1950s, Carter cut a series of consistently enjoyable small group recordings for Norman Granz's Verve label, including some with the house rhythm section, the Oscar Peterson Trio. They showcased Benny the performer rather than the arranger. Incredibly, the best session, with former Goodman pianist Teddy Wilson and Basie drummer Jo Jones, wasn't released until the 1990s (*3, 4, 5: The Verve Small Group Sessions*). Another excellent recording with Peterson is *Cosmopolite*, featuring the under-rated trombonist Bill Harris on some tracks.

Benny moved to the Contemporary label and in 1958 and made another fine record, *Jazz Giant*. It reunited him with Ben Webster, and they were backed by a roll call of west coast stars: pianists Andre Previn and Jimmy Rowles, guitarist Barney Kessel, bassist Leroy Vinnegar, and Shelly Manne on drums. In the liner notes, Nat Hentoff says: "Drive, heat, power and passion of logical invention – these are the qualities that are Benny Carter in this album". It is certainly superior to the over-praised *Further Definitions* from 1962 which never really sparks.

In later life, Benny became a very successful composer and arranger for movies and television. In the 1970s, he worked with pop singer Maria Muldaur. Carter continued to compose, perform and teach until the end. According to jazz writer Vic Bellerby, at the age of 94 Benny "resat (and passed) his driving test so he could drive one of his two Rolls Royce cars around Los Angeles – he was probably delivering film scores to Hollywood". Benny Carter died on 12 July 2003.

9. CHARLIE CHRISTIAN (1916-1942)

Charles Henry Christian was born in Oklahoma on 29 July 1916. Both his parents were professional musicians and Charlie went busking with his father and two brothers at an early age. At school, he made a guitar for himself from a cigar box. By the 1930s, Christian was playing smoking electric guitar and dazzling all who heard him.

The guitar in the early days of jazz was limited by its soft sound to the rhythm section or small groups. The development of amplification changed all this, but it took some time for a soloist to emerge who could exploit the new potential stylistically: Charlie Christian. Every guitarist that followed owes something to him. Christian played long, single string solos. The soft, full-bodied tone we associate with jazz guitar comes mainly from him. Critic Max Harrison has commented that Christian wove "a thread of the blues through all his music's fabric. There is a seeming paradox here in that his work is at the same time consistently modern, pointing towards bop … Despite their freedom of accentuation and sense of harmonic adventure, his best phrases have a logic, a simple inevitability, peculiarly their own" (M Harrison, C Fox and E Thacker, *The Essential Jazz Records: ragtime to swing*, Da Capo, 1988).

Jazz impresario John Hammond discovered Christian and brought him to Los Angeles in 1939 to join Benny Goodman – without asking Benny. Understandably taking umbrage, when Christian joined him on the stand for the first time, Goodman called for "Rose Room", thinking a hick from Oklahoma wouldn't know it. In fact, Charlie had played the song often. He improvised chorus after chorus in a performance that lasted three quarters of an hour. Benny hired him on the spot.

Although he also played with the big band, the majority of Christian's recorded output is with Goodman's sextet. It featured, in its various incarnations, Fletcher Henderson then Count Basie on piano, trumpeter "Cootie" Williams, Lionel Hampton on vibes, and drummers Jo Jones and Dave Tough. Charlie held his own with these seasoned pros effortlessly. Notable recordings are: "Flying Home", "Benny's Bugle", "Solo Flight" and "Air Mail Special".

In his brief career, Christian never recorded as a leader. Other than with Goodman, he recorded with New Orleans clarinettist Ed Hall in 1941 and was captured on some poor quality live recordings at Minton's Playhouse in Harlem, the birthplace of bebop.

Charlie Christian's career was cut tragically short. Tuberculosis exacerbated by hard living killed him on 2 March 1942 at the age of 25.

10. JOHN COLTRANE (1926-1967)

John William Coltrane was born on 23 September 1926 in North Carolina, moving to Philadelphia in his teens. Enlisting just before the end of the Second World War, "Trane" played alto sax in a Navy jazz band. After his discharge, he took up tenor and was profoundly influenced by bebop. Coltrane initially worked with Swing era bands, although he did a stint with "Dizzy" Gillespie, until he was hired by Miles Davis in 1955. Although critics rave about the Davis quintet's 1956 Prestige sessions (heresy to follow!), Coltrane was struggling to find his voice and translate his ideas into music and the results are sometimes ungainly and unformed.

An addictive and obsessive personality, Coltrane had serious alcohol and heroin problems at this time. Miles fired him in April 1957 as a result. It was a turning point. Returning to Philadelphia,

Coltrane had a profound spiritual reawakening. He renounced substance abuse and dedicated himself even more single-mindedly to his music. Some have attributed the strongly religious side of his nature to the fact that both his grandfathers were clergymen.

Soon after, Coltrane began working with Thelonious Monk. It was a fruitful partnership, particularly for Trane, as a live recording from Carnegie Hall in November 1957 shows. Stanley Crouch puts it well in his liner notes: "The thoroughness of Monk's self-confidence on the levels of melody, harmony, timbre and rhythm combined with Coltrane's fervour created a monumental fusion of intellect and soul".

In September 1957, Coltrane made his first great record, *Blue Train*, with trumpeter Lee Morgan and trombonist Curtis Fuller. His solo on the title track is a haunting, unearthly performance evoking "nightmarish images of a triumphant thrusting aside of endless barriers" (Michael James in M Harrison, A Morgan, R Atkins, M James, J Cooke eds, *Modern Jazz, 1945-70: the essential records*, Aquarius Books, 1975).

The cleaned-up Coltrane re-joined Miles in January 1958 and featured on a series of famous recordings, most notably *Kind of Blue*. He was now in full command of his music and its direction. In 1959, Trane recorded *Giant Steps*, a self-assured, mature work. With its lengthy, cascading solos, *Giant Steps* set the pattern for the future. No other jazz musician has been able to improvise so creatively for so long as Coltrane. The notes gush out like water bursting from a broken pipe. He also emerged as a significant composer, writing all the songs on the album. It was followed the next year by the equally ground-breaking *My Favourite Things*. On two tracks, Coltrane played soprano sax, an instrument previously synonymous with the 1930s. He produced beautiful sounds on this notoriously surly horn, which he played regularly from then on. Highlighting Trane's lyrical side, the title tune became a hit.

Coltrane signed with the Impulse label in 1961, beginning another period of fecund creativity. His first record for the new label was *Africa/Brass*, an intriguing big band session. His solo on "Blues Minor" should not be missed. In 1962 came a stunning record, *Live at the Village Vanguard*. Coltrane's solo on "Chasin' the Trane" was "swooping, twisting, roaring by turns, his sound filled with yawps and honks, cries and slurs". The effect was "so intense it battered down his listeners' defences, leaving them as exhilarated and nearly as drained as he was when he came to an end" (Ken Burns and Geoffrey Ward, *Jazz: a history of America's music*, Pimlico, 2001). *At the Village Vanguard* was re-released in a four CD complete edition in 1997.

In 1962 Coltrane formed his classic quartet. Pianist McCoy Tyner had a similar musical conception and the stamina and imagination to keep up during Trane's mammoth performances. Tyner's playing could be muscular or delicate as the occasion demanded. Drumming dervish Elvin Jones' powerful polyrhythms and crashing cymbals added to the excitement. Jimmy Garrison on bass completed this gathering of titans.

An excellent live recording, less challenging than the Vanguard set, is *Afro Blue Impressions*, recorded by the quartet on tour in Europe in 1963. It contains what is, to my mind, the definitive version of "My Favourite Things". Taken at a faster pace than the original, it is a 21 minute tour de force. When the ascending soprano solo finally ceases and Trane drops back to the melody, I remember to breathe again.

Increasingly, Coltrane's music became his personal religious vision. This reached its apotheosis in 1964 with *A Love Supreme*, a four part hymn of praise to God. To dissect this transcendent work is to do it a disservice. It communicates on every level: musical, intellectual, emotional, mystical. Listening to Coltrane's towering tenor is as awe-inspiring as standing in the nave of a medieval cathedral. His liner notes reveal the deeply spiritual nature of the music: "I would like to tell you that no matter what, it is with God. He is gracious and merciful. His way is through love, in which we all are. It is truly a love supreme. This album is a humble offering to Him. An attempt to say thank you God through our work".

Throughout his life, Coltrane had a compulsion to find new ways of making music. From 1965, he became involved in free jazz. Performances were lengthy, abstract, atonal and arrhythmic – one number could last for close to an hour. Alienated by the howling, tumultuous cacophony, audiences began to desert him, though not the critics.

Coltrane died of liver cancer on 17 July 1967. His final "cosmic" phase and early death ensured he would become a legend. San Francisco is home to the St John Coltrane African Orthodox Church. His legacy is not an unmixed one as he spawned a school of musicians who imitated the shrieking and groaning but lacked the musicality. Only someone of Coltrane's genius could bring off the extraordinary feats he attempted.

11. "SONNY" CRISS (1927-77)

Charlie Parker, the greatest bopper of them all, had a host of imitators. The over-rated Lou Donaldson made a career out of sounding like his idol. "Sonny" Stitt claimed to have invented bop at the same time as Parker but played with nothing like the master's artistry. He had a vinegary tone and a tendency to blast mindlessly through his solos. The other Sonny was influenced by Parker but built on his legacy to create an individual style. Criss was one of the best, although least known, of the post-Parker altoists.

William Criss was born in Memphis, Tennessee on 23 October 1927 and moved to Los Angeles as a teenager. He began playing alto sax before leaving high school and soon became prominent on the LA scene.

Sonny was spotted by jazz promoter Norman Granz, who asked him to join one of his famous (or perhaps one should say famously loud) Jazz at the Philharmonic tours. Sonny played "super-fast runs and soaring high register figures" with a "pure, urgent tone and delivery" (*Penguin Guide to Jazz*, 6th ed). He made some admirable records in the mid-1950s for the Imperial label reissued by Blue Note on a 2-CD set in 2000.

Criss' career was hampered by being a black bopper on the white west coast. He had trouble being noticed by the critics and even finding work. At one stage, frustrated with the LA scene, he spent some years in Europe. Sonny also had all too familiar personal problems. A heroin addict, he started drinking to get off the stuff and ended up an alcoholic junkie.

The best of Sonny's music comes from a late flowering. Producer Don Schlitten of east coast based Prestige Records had long been an admirer. In 1966, he flew Sonny to New York to record *This is Criss!* with an eminent ensemble: pianist Walter Davis, bassist Paul Chambers and drummer Alan Dawson. The cover stated, with only a touch of understandable hyperbole, "Here is an alto saxophonist whose consummate artistry approaches perfection".

The record revived Sonny's career and an even better one followed next year, *Portrait.* Criss could still do all the bop circus tricks but his playing now had great emotional depth and an aching, bluesy sound. Other notable recordings in the Prestige series were *Up, Up and Away,* featuring another neglected musician, guitarist Tal Farlow, and *I'll Follow the Sun,* with an ace west coast rhythm section of pianist Hamp Hawes, Monty Budwig on bass and Shelly Manne on drums. Unfortunately, Criss' time in the sun was brief. Diagnosed with stomach cancer, he shot himself on 19 November 1977.

12. MILES DAVIS (1926-1991)

Miles Davis played a role – often a major one – in every significant development in post-war jazz: bebop, the cool school, hard bop, modal improvisation, third stream (attempts to combine jazz and classical music), free bop, and jazz rock fusion. Throughout his career, Miles had a hunger for experimentation and innovation. Later in his life it degenerated into a fixation with fame and fashion.

Miles Dewey Davis was born on 26 May 1926 in Alton, Illinois. Unlike many jazz musicians, he had a privileged upbringing. His father was a dentist and the family were wealthy. Miles learnt trumpet from an early age. After completing high school, he studied music at the famous Juilliard School. Davis was soon seduced by the siren song of jazz and abandoned the classroom.

In 1945, Davis replaced "Dizzy" Gillespie in Charlie "Bird" Parker's quintet. Although struggling technically at times, he was an ideal foil for Bird. Miles' solos were more measured, a chance to re-enter the atmosphere after Parker's outer-space voyages. He was with Parker until 1948 and participated in some of the most famous jazz recordings ever made. Playing with Bird was the Harvard MBA of jazz and Miles graduated, although not without some collateral damage, such as a heroin habit.

In 1949, Davis changed track dramatically and made *The Birth of the Cool* with a group of west coast luminaries, chiefly Gerry Mulligan and Gil Evans. Although critically praised to the skies, I've always found it an unexciting record. Arrangements predominate, with the soloists playing as politely as if they are at grannie's tea party.

Between 1952 and 1954 Davis made some excellent sessions for Blue Note. Returning to his bop roots, he played hot, particularly on the 1954 session with Horace Silver, Percy Heath and Max Roach. There is also some lyrical ballad playing on "Enigma", "I Waited for You" and "Yesterdays". It was during this period that Miles kicked his heroin addiction, although drug and alcohol abuse remained a permanent feature of his lifestyle.

In mid-1954, Davis recorded *Walkin'* for Prestige Records. It is a hard bop masterpiece, with his mature style in place. Virtuosity was not Miles' strength, although his technical ability should not be discounted. Playing mainly in the middle register, he had a clean, ringing tone. *Walkin'* marked the emergence of Miles' use of the Harmon mute. Played close to the microphone, it produced a keening, intimate sound that became a hallmark.

Davis was in cracking form on a recording session on Christmas Eve 1954 with two other jazz giants: Thelonious Monk and Milt "Bags" Jackson. The circumstances surrounding the date are almost as famous as the music. Miles could be aloof, arrogant and aggressive. His evil temper and black moods led to him being nicknamed "the Prince of Darkness". On this occasion, Davis quarrelled with Monk, who could also be decidedly temperamental. Rumours spread that Miles had taken a swing at Thelonious. Both later debunked this, for the compelling reason that the bearish Monk would have beaten the slightly built Davis into smashed avocado. Whatever the details, the conflict seemed to spur the creativity. It was at this time that Miles became interested in, as he put it, "space breathing through the music". His lean, aerodynamic solo on an 11 minute version of "Bags Groove" reflects this. Monk's pianism is also sparse but in a more jagged way. Jackson's busy vibraphone solos provide a stimulating contrast.

Davis was offered a contract by Columbia in 1955 but owed Prestige some records. At the time, he was working with John Coltrane on tenor, pianist Red Garland, Paul Chambers on bass, and drummer "Philly" Joe Jones. Miles took the quintet into the studio and in a couple of marathon sessions cut enough to meet his obligations. In typical Prestige fashion, the music was dribbled out between 1956 and 1959 on four scrambled LPs. Most jazz books praise these records but to me the overall impression is of perfunctoriness. There is some good music, but many tracks have a "let's get it over with and get to the bar" feel. *Steamin'* is the pick of the bunch.

An immensely creative decade followed Davis' signing with Columbia. The new label promoted him heavily and invested a lot of money in his records, a wise decision as it turned out. In 1957, Miles collaborated with Gil Evans on *Miles Ahead.* Evans wrote the arrangements and conducted a 19 piece orchestra. His orchestrations were the perfect setting for Davis' 30 carat solos. Critic Max Harrison has said that the "elaboration and richness" of the scoring "surpassed everything previously achieved in orchestral jazz … Evans hits repeatedly on mixtures of sound that were new not only to jazz but to all orchestral music" (M Harrison, A Morgan, R Atkins, M James, J Cooke eds, *Modern Jazz, 1945-70: the essential records*, Aquarius Books, 1975). There were two further memorable collaborations, *Porgy and Bess* in 1958 and *Sketches of Spain* from 1960. The latter had a moody, yearning quality about it that increasingly typified Miles' music.

Davis also had a regular band, with Coltrane, altoist Julian "Cannonball" Adderley and the incomparable rhythm section of pianist Wynton Kelly, bassist Paul Chambers and Jimmy Cobb on drums. It was with this group, plus pianist Bill Evans (Kelly plays on one track only), that in March 1959 he made *Kind of Blue*. Miles asked the soloists to improvise on scales or modes, not chord progressions. It created an ethereal, eastern feel. *Kind of Blue* has been described as "three-quarters of an hour of extraordinary music loved equally by listeners who wouldn't know a mode from a modem, and by musicians for whom it seemed to point the way towards a fresh way of playing" (Ken Burns and Geoffrey Ward, *Jazz: a history of America's music*, Pimlico, 2001). A summation of the cerebral, evocative sound associated with Davis at the time, *Kind of Blue* became his most famous disc and the best-selling jazz record of all time.

By now, Miles was a celebrity, featuring in the gossip columns and fashion pages. In 1961, he was earning $150,000 a year. Still having a restless, relentless need to explore, Davis skimmed off the cream of up-and-coming young musicians to form a new quintet in 1964. Wayne Shorter was one of the best of the post-Coltrane tenors. No matter how unorthodox his solos, he was always compellingly listenable. Shorter also composed some memorable material for the group. Herbie Hancock was a fleet, expressive pianist influenced by Bill Evans. Ron Carter was "Mr Bass" – if you collected every record he appeared on you would have to buy a bigger house. Still in his teenage years, Tony Williams showed that even after Blakey, Jones and Roach a drummer could say new things. This band's astonishing debut was *Miles in Berlin*, a live recording consisting of introspective versions of "Autumn Leaves" and "Stella by Starlight" plus numbers from the standard Davis repertoire played with new complexity.

Four magnificent studio albums followed: *ESP*, *Miles Smiles*, *Sorcerer* and *Nefertiti*. The style was aptly dubbed free bop. Although all members of the group played with considerable freedom the music never entirely breaks away from a grounding in bop rhythm and harmony. A feature of the quintet was the "huge creative tension between Shorter's oblique, churning solos and the leader's private musings". Miles returned to "his old tactic with Coltrane of paring away steadily. He does not solo on *Nefertiti*, one of the great compositions from this time, on which the horns simply pace away over Williams' boiling rhythm" (*Penguin Guide to Jazz*, 6th ed). The quintet's innovativeness and intensity are captured in concert on *The Complete Live at the Plugged Nickel 1965*, an eight CD set released in 1995.

The second quintet was more of an artistic than commercial success. By the late 1960s, Davis' popularity was fading and his sales falling. Obsessed with staying a star, he moved into rock and funk. This was first evident on the over-rated *In a Silent Way* from 1969, which featured rock guitarist John McLaughlin. It consists of two long, meandering tracks that never develop into anything resembling jazz. The album would be more accurately titled "In an Aimless Way".

Davis moved further and further away from jazz and more and more into money, glitz, superstardom – and superficiality. Respected jazz critic Martin Williams has described him in a late performance as "stalking around a stage in what looked like a left-over Halloween fright suit, emitting a scant handful of plaintive notes".

Miles Davis died on 28 September 1991 of the combined effects of a stroke, pneumonia, and respiratory failure.

13. KENNY DORHAM (1924-1972)

McKinley Howard "Kenny" Dorham was born in Fairfield, Texas on 30 August 1924, and was playing piano at age seven. In high school, Kenny divided his time between boxing and jazz trumpet. Music won out, and he worked with a number of bands, including that of "Dizzy" Gillespie, before replacing Miles Davis in Charlie Parker's quintet.

Dorham was an inventive soloist with an exciting attack who sparkled without being shrill. Critic Bob Blumenthal described his sound as "tight but full-toned, and chipping away into hurt at the edges". After Gillespie, "Fats" Navarro and Clifford Brown, Dorham was at the top of the next division. He was also a talented composer. Sadly, Kenny never achieved the recognition he deserved. This was due partly to bad luck and partly to the fact that, unlike Miles, he lacked the streak of aggressiveness necessary to succeed in a tough environment. Dorham was also plagued by debilitating kidney disease in his final years. Much of his later music does have a tinge of melancholy.

In 1955, Dorham was an original member of that archetypal hard bop band the Jazz Messengers, with Art Blakey and Horace Silver. The next year, Kenny started his own group, the Jazz Prophets. In the front line was another under-rated musician, tenor player JR Monterose (not to be confused with west coast tenor Jack Montrose). JR had recently featured on Charlie Mingus' classic LP *Pithecanthropus Erectus*. Unfortunately, the band folded after a year, but a live recording from May 1956, *Round about Midnight* at the Cafe Bohemia, shows what a great outfit it was. A future Jazz Messenger, Bobby Timmons, was on piano, and the ubiquitous Kenny Burrell on guitar – he was to the guitar what Tommy Flanagan was to the piano. Dorham "always had a predilection for a unified mood" and on this session he sustains "a slightly brooding, intensely thoughtful atmosphere" (*Penguin Guide to Jazz*, 6th ed).

When Clifford Brown was tragically killed in a car accident in 1956, Max Roach hired Dorham as his replacement. Sonny Rollins and then Hank Mobley were on tenor. Kenny played on some of Roach's best hard bop records, coping effortlessly with the leader's machine gun-like drum breaks. Dorham's extended solo on "Valse Hot" from *Jazz in ¾ Time* is masterly. A progression of pithy phrases builds into a perfectly structured whole.

In 1959, Dorham made *Quiet Kenny* with a talented ensemble: Tommy Flanagan on piano, Paul Chambers on bass, and drummer Art Taylor. It showcased the lyrical, wistful side of his playing. Another fine record was *Whistle Stop* from 1961. Kenny wrote all the material. It has been described as the epitome of Dorham's mature style:

> His tone, for instance, has always been one of his strong points, staggering at times in its polish and purity; with the passage of time he had become a true virtuoso in this area … Harmonically, too, he has grown bolder … However, it is Dorham the composer as much as Dorham the improviser that this record sets out to define; and it does so with equal success (Michael James in M Harrison, A Morgan, R Atkins, M James, J Cooke eds, *Modern Jazz, 1945-70: the essential records*, Aquarius Books, 1975).

Dorham had always been keen to foster the careers of talented, young musicians and in the 1960s teamed up with new tenor star Joe Henderson. Rather than being uncomfortable with late bop players, Kenny responded with fresh depths of intensity. In a productive partnership, they made some excellent records, notably *Page One* and *Our Thing* from 1963.

In the jazz downturn of the late 1960s, Kenny could no longer sustain a full-time musical career and worked at various day jobs. He spent much time in Europe where he was more appreciated. Dorham died of kidney failure on 5 December 1972 at the age of 48.

14. "DUKE" ELLINGTON (1899-1974)

Now we come to the pinnacle, the greatest of the great: "Duke" Ellington. Percy Grainger was one of the first to recognise Duke's genius. When Grainger was Professor of Music at New York University, he invited Ellington in October 1932 to perform as part of a lecture series he was giving. Grainger introduced him by saying: "The three greatest composers who ever lived are Bach, Delius and Duke Ellington. Unfortunately, Bach is dead, Delius is very ill, but we are happy to have with us today the Duke".

Much time has been spent analysing Ellington's music – solid tomes roll off the presses regularly – but there is something indefinably special at its heart. While writing this entry, I was binge listening to Duke. I had to stop as it was taking over: bits of Ellingtonia hummed ceaselessly through my mind.

Edward Kennedy "Duke" Ellington was born in Washington, DC on 29 April 1899. His parents were among the better-off in the city's black population and were amateur pianists. A school friend nick-named him Duke because of his aristocratic manner. He took formal lessons in piano and music. Informally, Ellington was influenced by stride pianists such as James P Johnson and "Fats" Waller. He dropped out of high school, where he was studying commercial art, and started working as a jazz musician.

In 1923, Duke decided to leave Washington behind and take on New York. He led a band called the Washingtonians and played regularly at the Kentucky Club. Ellington began to make a name for himself, assisted by the public relations skills of music publisher Irving Mills who became his manager. With the assistance of Mills, Duke recorded prolifically.

Ellington's career really took off when he was hired in 1927 by the Cotton Club, a popular night spot in New York. A representative of the gangsters who owned the club, "Yankee" Schwartz, went to see the manager of the theatre in Philadelphia where Duke was under contract to ask for his release. The message was simple: "Be big, be big or be dead". The Ellington band was immediately available.

An all-white audience went to the Cotton Club for the African experience, including attractive, light-coloured show girls. Duke supplied "jungle music", featuring trumpeter "Bubber" Miley who used a plunger mute to create guttural, growling solos. As Stanley

Dance has noted, Miley often displayed more enthusiasm for wine and women than for song. Heavy drinking led to his departure from the band after a few years and premature death in 1932. However, Bubber's legacy was passed on to a succession of Ellington brass players.

Ellington's precocity was extraordinary. By the late 1920s he had recorded some unforgettable masterpieces: "East St Louis Toodle-oo", "Creole Love Call", "Black and Tan Fantasy", "The Mooche". Duke had also gathered around him a group of exceptional musicians, many of whom would stay with him for decades: clarinettist Barney Bigard, trumpeter "Cootie" Williams, trombonist "Tricky Sam" Nanton, drummer "Sonny" Greer. Then there were what jazz scholar Dan Morgenstern describes as the "three constants": Harry Carney on baritone, "the incomparable anchor of the reeds"; Johnny Hodges, "the matchless poet of the alto sax"; and Lawrence Brown, "the grand romantic of the trombone". Bassist Wellman Braud was a key figure, as the Ellington band was driven more by the bass than the drums. Greer's role was more that of percussionist, with a spectacular drum kit worth $3,000.

The main elements of Ellington's style were already present: compositional brilliance; weaving the skills of his soloists into the fabric of the music; and the creation of tone poems – or tone parallels to use the term Duke coined. He took lessons in orchestration and listened to Delius, Debussy and Ravel. The result was a unique blend of powerful swing, subtle nuances, tonal colour, and innovative arrangements.

Ellington has been criticised for taking his musicians' ideas and not giving them sufficient credit. While there is some truth in this, it should not be exaggerated or allowed to diminish his overall achievement. To use a political analogy, while the speech writer crafts the words, the leader has the ultimate responsibility for delivering and implementing them. Adam Gopnik in the *New Yorker* (23-30 December 2013) provided this balanced assessment: "Ellington really did take other men's ideas and act as if they were his own. But he did this because he took other men's ideas and made them his own. There are artists whose genius lies in exploiting other people's talent, and we can recognize the exploitation as the genius". Gopnik asks whether any of the band members would have had "the energy and mastery to form a band, sustain it, recruit the right musicians, survive their eccentricities and addictions, give them music they could play, record it, and keep enough of a popular audience alive to justify the expense of the rest?"

Ellington once described his band as "eighteen maniacs". Unlike Benny Goodman, he was extremely tolerant of his musicians' foibles. Duke usually opened concerts with a piano solo, "Kinda Dukish", to give wayward members of the band time to get on stage. However, he exerted a subtle discipline. If someone showed up late or drunk, Duke would wait for the right moment then tear into a number and make the offender play chorus after chorus.

One member of the band who never received as much exposure as he should have is the pianist. As has been said, even if Ellington did nothing but play the piano he would still have been famous. His style was multi-faceted. Duke's beginnings were in Harlem stride and he had a strong left hand until the end. He often played in a sparse, angular way, anticipating Thelonious Monk. Some of Ellington's solos were impressionistic miniatures. He could also produce flowing, lyrical improvisations, a feature of some of his later recordings. It is a mystery as to why Duke made so little of his instrumental talent and, when he did, often gave the impression of not taking it very seriously, for example, on the unsatisfactory record he made with Louis Armstrong in 1961.

There isn't a lot of worthwhile Ellington piano on record, although *Piano Reflections* from 1953 and *Piano in the Foreground* from 1961 are both excellent. *Money Jungle* (1962) with Max Roach and Charlie Mingus put Duke into an inappropriate stylistic context. Mingus, in particular, seems to be saying: I'm really goin' to make the old guy work. *Live at the Whitney*, recorded in 1972 but not released until 1995, is a sample of late Ducal pianism. In 2005, the Storyville label compiled Ellington solos from the 1960s and 70s into a worthwhile album, including a piano version of his ballet suite *The River*.

Ellington's four year residency at the Cotton Club, combined with regular nationwide radio broadcasts, made him one of the best-known band leaders in the US. As well as the music, there was the Duke himself: handsome, cosmopolitan, witty, with a winning smile and engaging manner. Sonny Greer observed: "I've never seen another man like him. When he walks into a strange room, the whole place lights up". Duke had a natural dignity that he maintained in spite of the slights and humiliations American racism inflicted on him. Out of the spotlight, he was an intensely private person who few, if any, really knew.

In 1933-34, Duke had a hugely successful tour of Britain and France, with sell-out concerts and rapturous audiences. In London, the Prince of Wales (the future King Edward VIII) sat in on drums. British composer Constant Lambert, son of Australian artist George and father of the Who's manager Kit, said:

> After hearing what Ellington can do with 14 players, the average modern composer who splashes about with 80 players in

the Respighi manner must feel a little chastened. All this is clearly apparent to anyone who visits the Palladium, but what may not be so apparent is that Ellington is no mere band leader and arranger but a composer of uncommon merit, probably the first composer of real character to come out of America.

Ellington continued to reach new highs, recording classic after classic throughout the 1930s: "Ring Dem Bells", "Mood Indigo", "Rockin' in Rhythm", "It Don't Mean a Thing (If it Ain't Got that Swing)", "Sophisticated Lady", "Solitude", "In A Sentimental Mood", "Caravan". There were also some remarkable extended works, "Creole Rhapsody", "Diminuendo and Crescendo in Blue", and the 12 minute "Reminiscing In Tempo" from 1935. British classical and jazz critic Max Harrison has said that the last is

> in its structural ambitions, unlike any other American jazz of the period and a notable demonstration of Ellington's independence of mind. A main point is the level of formal elaboration – the simple frameworks that are suitable vehicles for improvisation being abandoned with a certainty of purpose, almost a ruthlessness, that still seems remarkable. 'Reminiscing in Tempo' remains his most adventurous piece, the furthest out that he went (M Harrison, C Fox and E Thacker, *The Essential Jazz Records: ragtime to swing*, Da Capo, 1988).

Duke began to write mini concertos for his favourite soloists: Rex Stewart, Cootie Williams, Lawrence Brown, and Barney Bigard. Probably the best is "Clarinet Lament" from 1936. Bigard had a woody, New Orleans sound that Duke particularly liked. Max Harrison has described his solo as "one of the finest recorded expressions of specifically jazz lyricism and virtuosity for clarinet".

Many believe that the greatest of all the Ellington outfits is that of the early 1940s. The band and Duke personally were at the height of their powers. Although Bigard and Williams had departed (the latter to return in the 1960s), a fresh group of maestros was on board: clarinettist Jimmy Hamilton (who also played tenor sax); trumpeters Ray Nance (who doubled effectively on violin) and "Cat" Anderson (famous for his powerful high note crescendos up to triple C). Ben Webster on tenor saxophone was a major new voice who could wail or sound soft and sensuous. Webster brought the reed section up to five, giving it parity with the brass, a characteristic of the later Ducal sound. Bassist Jimmy Blanton's technical and musical prowess gave the band a new rhythmic vitality. Sadly, Blanton died of tuberculosis in 1942. Ellington had probably his best ever vocalist in Ivie Anderson, who also died prematurely, in 1949.

The Ellington orchestra was greatly strengthened by the arrival of Billy Strayhorn in 1939. He quickly became Duke's closest collaborator. "Strays" and Duke were personally an unlikely couple: "Strayhorn was warm, gregarious and openly homosexual in a time when most gay people remained grimly closeted. Ellington was private, enigmatic, and a flamboyant ladies' man". However, they were almost telepathically compatible when it came to music. Ellington described Strayhorn as "my right arm, my left arm, all the eyes in the back of my head; my brainwaves are in his head, and his in mine" (Ken Burns and Geoffrey Ward, *Jazz: a history of America's music*, Pimlico, 2001). Strayhorn co-composed with Duke, wrote his own songs, and arranged most of the non-Ellington material. On occasion, he sat in for Duke on piano.

This band can be heard in all its glory on a live recording made at Fargo, North Dakota on 7 November 1940. It is thanks to two young Ellington fans who were audio enthusiasts that it exists. They hooked up microphones on stage to a portable, battery-powered acetate disc cutter and captured two hours of the band at its peak in remarkable sound quality. The cats sound relaxed, stretching out on numbers rather than being confined to the three minute limit of the studio.

The 1940s Ellington studio recordings were of astonishingly high quality, even for him: "Ko-Ko", "In a Mellotone", "Cotton Tail", "Never No Lament" (with lyrics added retitled "Don't Get Around Much Anymore"), "Sepia Panorama", "Take the A Train", "Sentimental Lady", "I Got It Bad and that Ain't Good", "Perdido", "Chelsea Bridge", "C Jam Blues". Assessing the 1940s Ducal output, Dan Morgenstern poses the question: "Is there any other band that had so many strings to its bow, so many hues in its tonal palette? The answer, needless to say, is a resounding no. There never was, and never will be, another band like Duke Ellington and his Famous Orchestra".

In the late 1940s, Ellington gave a series of annual concerts at Carnegie Hall. The recordings were not released until the 1970s as the sound quality was so awful. At the first concert, in 1943, Duke premiered a 45-minute work, *Black, Brown and Beige*, subtitled *A tone parallel to the history of the Negro in America*. Disconcerted by the negative reaction from jazz and classical critics, he never played it again in its entirety and turned away from composition on this scale. Ellington always had a dynamic, work-in-progress attitude to his music: try it out and if it doesn't work – and there were occasions when it didn't – move on.

In 1944, Ellington recorded an 18 minute version of *Black, Brown and Beige*. In 1958, he fashioned two of the themes, "Work Song" and "Come Sunday", into an LP featuring gospel singer Mahalia Jackson. She is particularly powerful on "Come Sunday" and the 23rd Psalm which concludes the disc. Duke went on to write many suites (usually with Strayhorn), but these were collections of songs around a theme without the formal structure of a classical work.

In spite of the lack of success of *Black, Brown and Beige* at the time, Duke is the only jazz musician to enter the classical repertoire as a composer. There is a growing body of his work recorded by major orchestras. In 2012, for example, the Buffalo Philharmonic under prominent American conductor JoAnn Falletta recorded an all-Ellington disc, including *Black, Brown and Beige*.

In the early 1950s, with big bands out of fashion, Ellington's career was languishing. However, he staged a dramatic revival at the 1956 Newport jazz festival. The orchestra boasted some new stars: trumpeter Clark Terry, who brought a bebop influence to the band, and the magnificent tenor saxophonist, Paul Gonsalves. Johnny Hodges returned in 1955 after some years leading his own outfit. He was, arguably, the greatest of the Duke's men, excelling at both smooth, silky sounds and swinging blues.

Ellington knew that all eyes would be on Newport and was determined to use the occasion to show he still had plenty to give. The moment came when he called for "Diminuendo and Crescendo in Blue". Duke normally played a bridge between the two sections but instead put on Gonsalves who played 27 consecutive choruses. Producer George Avakian described what happened:

> At about his seventh chorus, the tension which had been building both on stage and in the audience since Duke kicked off the piece, suddenly broke. A platinum blonde girl in a black dress began dancing in one of the boxes. Throughout the rest of the performance there were frequent bursts of wild dancing and literally acres of people stood on their

chairs cheering and clapping. I had a rare view of the audience (about 7,000 were still there, about midnight on the last night). Halfway through Paul's solo, it had become an enormous living organism, reacting like waves in ripples to the music played before it.

Duke was back: Columbia signed him within days, he made the cover of *Time* magazine, *Ellington at Newport* became his best-selling album. There was, however, an intriguing, behind-the-scenes story about the LP, not revealed until Phil Schaap's meticulous re-issue in 1999. CBS was unhappy with the sound quality and the band went into the studio to re-create parts of the concert which, with crowd noise added, made up much of the initial release. Schaap found the original Columbia tape plus a recording by Voice of America thought to have been lost. He combined both to restore the actual Ellington performance in stereo.

Ellington's music had more scope and sophistication in the 1950s. As always, he was trying out new ideas. His audience had also changed, from Swing era rug-cutters to cool hipsters. One of Duke's most famous recordings from this era is *Such Sweet Thunder* released in 1957. As the *Penguin Guide to Jazz* (6th ed) says: "The wit and sagacity of his nod to Will Shakespeare makes for one of the most delightful of all Ellington records. Sweet, swinging, perfect Ellingtonia". *Blues in Orbit* from 1959 is another high point. A small gem, less well known, is *The Queen's Suite*. In 1958, Duke was presented to Queen Elizabeth II, stalling the reception line while he flirted (mildly) with her. The next year he and Strayhorn wrote *The Queen's Suite*, which Ellington recorded at his own expense. He had just one copy pressed and sent it to HM. It remained unreleased until after his death.

Duke entered the 1960s in good form, as a Paris concert from 1963 makes clear. It is, in some ways, a summation of his past achievement. Ellington loved Paris and "the city of light" loved him. The band is playing at its peak. Johnny Hodges has some typical lush ballad features – "Star-Crossed Lovers", "All of Me" – and swings through "Things Ain't What They Used to Be" as only he could. Cootie Williams, who had just re-joined, plays as well as ever on "Concerto for Cootie", "Tutti for Cootie" and "Echoes of Harlem". Lawrence Brown displays to the full his fluent, mellow trombone style on "Rose of the Rio Grande". There are performances of "The Blues" from *Black, Brown and Beige* and the infectiously jaunty "Happy-Go-Lucky Local" from the 1946 *Deep South Suite*. Above all, two suites are performed in their entirety, *Sweet Thursday* (named after John Steinbeck's novel) and *A Tone Parallel to Harlem*, commissioned by Arturo Toscanini for the NBC Symphony Orchestra in 1950.

Ellington's last decade was marked by the creation of some remarkable suites. A number were inspired by overseas travel, as the State Department began sponsoring tours by the band – possibly America's wisest foreign policy decision of the era. After his first visit to Asia and the Middle East, Ellington released the *Far East Suite* in 1966. Of the impressions he absorbed, Duke said: "You let it roll around, undergo a chemical change, and then seep out on paper in the form that will suit the musicians who are going to play it". It seeped out as one of his finest achievements. Each song evokes mystery and majesty. Gonsalves' brooding tenor dominates many of the pieces; Hodges excels on "Isfahan", one of Ellington and Strayhorn's most emotive compositions; a snatch of bird song heard by Strayhorn forms the basis of Jimmy Hamilton's clarinet solo on "Bluebird of Delhi"; Duke plays impassioned piano on "Tourist Point of View" and "Ad Lib on Nippon".

A tour south of the border in 1968 resulted in the *Latin American Suite*. That most perceptive of Ellington commentators, Stanley Dance, has noted that it is

> not an attempt to re-interpret the musical forms indigenous to the countries Duke visited; it reproduces musically the impressions made on him by those countries and their peoples. A striking difference between this and his other suites is in the much greater emphasis on the ensemble and the piano player's role. For once, most of the other soloists take second place.

Ellington was never formulaic. While other band leaders of his era were trading on their reputation and nostalgia, Duke continued to explore, innovate and develop.

The grim reaper became a follower of the band. Strayhorn died of leukaemia in 1967. Duke recorded an album of his compositions as a tribute, *And His Mother Called Him Bill*. Strayhorn was composing until the end, as the titles of two tracks indicate, "Blood Count" and "UMMG" (Upper Manhattan Medical Group). There are alternate versions of one of Strayhorn's most beautiful melodies, "Lotus Blossom". Duke first plays it solo then in a trio with bassist Aaron Bell and Harry Carney. The second version, with Carney's starkly emotional baritone playing, remained unissued for 20 years but to me is the more moving. Johnny Hodges died suddenly in 1970 while the band was recording the *New Orleans Suite*. A series of portraits of the city and the creators of jazz such as Louis Armstrong and Sidney Bechet, it was the last great work. Duke Ellington died of lung cancer and pneumonia on 24 May 1974.

15. BILL EVANS (1929-1980)

After Earl "Bud" Powell, who invented bop piano, Bill Evans was the most influential jazz pianist in the second half of the 20th century and beyond. Keith Jarrett, McCoy Tyner, Herbie Hancock and a multitude of others are indebted to him. Evans had technical agility, an introspective, lyrical style, and a new harmonic language. Evans' enormous popularity has been attributed to two factors:

His records were widely disseminated and listened to by musicians, and their attractive surface also appealed to an audience seeking sophisticated but easy-going new jazz. He suggested to more than one generation of pianists a way of dealing with modality, and his harmonic thinking showed a subtle way out of the dead-end of bebop changes (*Penguin Guide to Jazz*, 6th ed).

The creator of this unearthly music had a very earthy personal life: he was a heroin and cocaine addict. Jazz writer Terry Teachout has observed:

> Sometimes a musician embodies a contradiction, and then you can read it off his face, just as you can see a fault line snaking through a tranquil landscape. Such was the case with Bill Evans. His shining tone and cloudy pastel harmonies transformed such innocuous pop songs as "Young and Foolish" and "The Boy Next Door" into fleeting visions of infinite grace. Yet the bespectacled, cadaverous ruin who sat hunched over the keyboard like a broken gooseneck lamp seemed at first glance incapable of such Debussyan subtlety; something, one felt sure, must have gone terribly wrong for a man who played like that to have looked like that (*New York Times*, 13 September 1998).

William John Evans was born on 16 August 1929 in New Jersey. His childhood was unsettled as his father, who ran a golf course, was a drunk and a gambler. Evans studied music at Southeastern Louisiana University, playing Beethoven's third piano concerto for his graduation recital. Soon after, he began working professionally as a jazz musician.

Evans was influenced by Bud Powell, but also by Lennie Tristano, who offered the only stylistic alternative to bebop at the time. Blind from an early age, Lennie was an eccentric genius with a virtuosic technique. His musical philosophy emphasised intellect over emotion. Nothing was to distract from the quality of the improvisation. Bill was his own man, however. He refined his style by "discarding the more obvious flights of virtuosity. Those fulsome Lennie Tristano-like runs with their oblique accents and cross-rhythms lost their somewhat mechanised air as the lyricist in Evans took complete charge" (Ronald Atkins in M Harrison, A Morgan, R Atkins, M James, J Cooke eds, *Modern Jazz, 1945-70: the essential records*, Aquarius Books, 1975).

Evans' first recording under his own name was *New Jazz Conceptions*, released by Riverside in 1956. It was a little more boppish than future albums but contained a memorable blues, "No Cover, No Minimum", and some delightful solo vignettes. Riverside owner and producer Orrin Keepnews remembered that it had "wonderful reviews and no sales" (*Telegraph*, UK, 22 September 2007).

The big break came when Evans was invited to join Miles Davis' sextet in 1958 and played on the famous *Kind of Blue* album. Davis commented: "Bill had this quiet fire that I loved on piano. The way he approached it, the sound he got was like crystal notes or sparkling water cascading down from some clear waterfall".

Keepnews has said that Evans suffered from "a paralysing combination of perfectionism and self-doubt". It took him over two years to entice Evans, who claimed he had nothing new to say, into the studio again. The result was the masterly *Everybody Digs Bill Evans* with bassist Sam Jones and drummer "Philly" Joe Jones (*Telegraph*, UK, 22 September 2007).

Evans worked with a trio for most of his career and in 1959 formed the most famous of them, with Paul Motian on drums and the gifted Scott La Faro on bass. This group's first recording was *Portrait in Jazz*, arguably Evans' finest album. Critic Ronald Atkins has commented: "Evans no longer attempts to overwhelm us. His touch has grown lighter and just that bit more controlled; each phrase, each note, is given the finest dynamic shading. Confidence in his timing enables him to make a more subtle use of space between phrases and to bring off the most dazzling rhythmic displacements almost as an afterthought" (M Harrison, A Morgan, R Atkins, M James, J Cooke eds, *Modern Jazz, 1945-70: the essential records*, Aquarius Books, 1975). The trio's follow up, *Explorations*, was almost as good.

In 1961, Evans recorded a live set at the Village Vanguard. By now, La Faro had almost equal prominence in the front line – in my heretical opinion a mixed blessing, as I have always been dubious about the bass as a solo instrument. Tedious, over-lengthy solos by mediocre bassists are the unfortunate legacy of the Evans trio – it's normally when I go to the fridge to get another beer. None of this is to disparage La Faro's ability; however, a little goes a long way. The complete Vanguard recordings were released as a three CD set in 2005. The event has gained a certain mystique from the tragic death of La Faro in a road accident soon after.

It was not until mid-1962 that Evans recorded again. The results were issued on two separate LPs, *Moon Beams*, a ballad collection, and the more up tempo *How My Heart Sings!* His new bassist was Chuck Israels, a much less dominant player than La Faro. Joe Goldberg has perceptively noted in his liner notes that the

> muscular force that made Evans' up-tempo work as a sideman so notable has now become an integral part of his ballad playing, giving him the delicate strength of silk thread. Whether or not this is due to Israels' presence is, of course, a matter of sheer speculation, but the new quality is there, and it makes Evans a more impressive pianist than he has ever been.

Evans left Riverside in 1963 for a major label, Norman Granz's Verve. According to Orrin Keepnews, Evans was driven by his heroin habit to make "financial requests that were very difficult for us as a small, struggling record company, to deal with" (*Telegraph*, UK, 22 September 2007).

To fulfil his contractual obligations, Evans recorded a solo piano session in January 1963. It was not a happy occasion. Keepnews recalls that Bill was "tense, withdrawn, possibly strung-out, almost certainly full of misgivings about where and how he was going. I was equally uncool. I found it quite distressing that this was to be my last sight from the control room of Bill Evans at work". Because of the negative emotions surrounding the date, it was not issued at the time and Keepnews subsequently forgot about the tapes. He came upon them after Evans' death and "belatedly recognised them for the masterpieces they are". They were released in 1983 in two volumes as *The Solo Sessions*.

Evans never again achieved the consistent brilliance and vitality of his Riverside period but still made some memorable records. On *Conversations with Myself* he experimented with over-dubbing, something pioneered by Lennie Tristano. It's not a complete success as, to my ears, the three piano tracks sometimes create an unpleasant, jangling effect. Better, though less well known, is the follow up, *Further Conversations*, from 1967. The two pianos meld seamlessly to create a satisfying performance. In 1978, Evans returned to the concept and recorded *New Conversations*. This one is ruled completely out of court because, for some reason, he plays an electric piano. The tinny sound clashes with the beautiful tone of the acoustic instrument.

Bill released an excellent solo album, *Alone*, in 1968. In the revealing liner notes he says:

> Despite the fact that I am a professional performer, it is true that I have always preferred playing without an audience. This has nothing to do with my desire to communicate or not, but

rather I think just a problem of personal self-consciousness which had to be conquered through discipline and concentration. Yet, to know one is truly alone with one's instrument and music has always been an attractive and conducive situation for me to find my best playing level. What I desired to present in a solo piano recording was especially this unique feeling.

He succeeded. The 1975 sequel, *Alone (Again)*, is a high point of Evan's later output. His playing on an extended version of "People" is exquisite.

Evans formed a productive partnership with guitarist Jim Hall, who also had a subtle, lyrical style. Hall was a west coast musician but could swing and was a sought-after accompanist, working with saxophonists as widely divergent as Sonny Rollins and Jimmy Giuffre. Hall and Evans made two celebrated duo records. Most critics have put *Undercurrent*, released in 1962, ahead of *Intermodulation*, recorded four years later, but I score it the other way. Annotator James Isaacs argues that *Intermodulation*'s "repertoire and pacing, plus the contributions of Hall are superior". He describes it as "a softly glowing gem, for its radiance does not blind, but reflects the subtle brilliance of two master craftsmen".

Evans' output in the seventies was, on the whole, pleasant but predictable. The *Penguin Guide* puts it politely: "Consistency had become Evans' long suit, and he seemed content to tinker endlessly with his favourite pieces, disclosing little beyond the beauty of his touch". Exceptions were *You Must Believe in Spring* (1977) and the *Paris Concert* (1979) where Evans seems to recapture much of his old mastery. To quote TS Eliot, "The music succeeds with a dying fall". Bill Evans died on 15 September 1980 of a combination of a stomach ulcer, pneumonia, cirrhosis and hepatitis.

16. TOMMY FLANAGAN (1930-2001)

Thomas Lee Flanagan was born in Detroit on 16 March 1930. His parents were music-lovers and encouraged him to play at an early age. Tommy started on clarinet but switched to piano at 11. Detroit had a thriving jazz scene at the time. Prominent local players included pianists Hank Jones, Roland Hanna and Barry Harris, vibes player Milt Jackson, and guitarist Kenny Burrell. It also had a renowned jazz club, the Bluebird. So, when Tommy came of age he didn't have to go far to find work and was never short of it.

In 1956, Flanagan moved to New York and into the heart of the bebop scene. On occasion, he sat in for "Bud" Powell in nightclub performances. His first date on his own, *Overseas*, recorded in in 1957, was a fairly straight-forward bop album. Three years later came a very different trio album for the Moodsville label. It was a smooth, low-key set of ballad performances. And there we have two of the three sides of Flanagan.

First is the hard-hitting bop pianist. British critic Roy Carr accurately lists as the "classic grand-standing tenor with rhythm workouts", John Coltrane's *Giant Steps*, Sonny Rollin's *Saxophone Colossus*, J R Monterose's *The Message*, Hank Mobley's *Soul Station*, and *Introducing Johnny Griffin*. Who played piano on the first three but Tommy Flanagan? (Another unsung hero, Wyn Kelly, was on the last two). When Wes Montgomery came to New York in 1960 to record, Riverside Records owner and producer Orrin Keepnews decided to match him with "a tough eastern rhythm section", including, of course, Flanagan.

Then there is Tommy the *Jazz Poet*, as his excellent 1989 album was entitled. Elegant, lyrical, urbane are adjectives often used to describe his playing. Flanagan's sound was supple and caressing but there was strength and clarity at its core. He was dexterous without being overly demonstrative. Jazz critic John Fordham has noted that Tommy "liked to unfold a melody in chords, suspending the thematic momentum before a solo with a gleeful single line prevarication, then sweeping into a series of choruses full of glossy, tumbling arpeggios" (*Guardian*, 20 November 2001).

Flanagan's third life was as a sideman and accompanist. A master of the latter role, Tommy saw it as legitimate in itself. This is a given in classical music but in jazz the accompanist was often regarded as a secondary figure. Tommy accompanied Ella Fitzgerald from 1962-65 and 1968-78, and worked with Tony Bennett in 1966. John Fordham has said about Tommy's innumerable dates accompanying others: "He frequently led the listener to ask 'Who the hell was that?' He was the sideman who consistently stopped you from going to make the tea when the main attraction wasn't playing" (*Guardian*, 20 November 2001).

From the 1970s onwards, Flanagan began to record more under his own name. He preferred to work in the trio format, for many years with Czech bassist George Mraz. Ben Ratliff in the *New York Times* said of the trio's work:

> A sense of self-restraint permeated all the band's performances, with solo breaks that were not too long and all ideas tastefully wrapped up; the melody line never disappeared under his improvisations. Flanagan's touch and rhythmic bounce connoted the spontaneity of jazz, and yet the shape of his playing gave evidence he could see a map of the entire piece (19 November 2001)

Recommended trio recordings are: *Plays the Music of Harold Arlen, Magnificent, Thelonica, Nights at the Vanguard, Jazz Poet, Lady Be Good ... For Ella.*

Unfortunately, Flanagan rarely recorded solo. He did, however, produce the splendid *Alone Too Long* in 1977. Two other rewarding solo discs are *In his Own Sweet Way* (1994) and *Solo Piano* (recorded in 1974 but not released until 2005). Tommy teamed up with Hank Jones, a pianist who shared many of his virtues, to make two enjoyable duo albums, *Our Delights* and *I'm All Smiles* – what else would you be after playing a set like that? A more unorthodox but equally satisfying duo album was a reunion with saxophonist JR Monterose, *A Little Pleasure.*

Tommy had a heart attack in 1978, a factor in his giving up touring with Ella Fitzgerald, and in 1991 underwent quadruple bypass surgery. Nonetheless, he maintained a punishing playing and recording schedule. A softly spoken, reserved man, Flanagan was inflexible about maintaining the integrity of his art. He died of an arterial aneurism on 16 November 2001.

17. STAN GETZ (1927-1991)

Stanley Gayetski was born in Philadelphia on 2 February 1927. His family were Russian Jewish emigrants who changed their name to Getz. Stan was academically gifted but music was his passion. He began playing tenor at 13 and was so precociously talented that three years later he joined Jack Teagarden's band. Because of his age, "Big T" became Stan's legal guardian. The hard-drinking Teagarden was not exactly a good example for a young man and Getz became a life-long alcoholic.

Stan was also addicted to heroin. In 1954, he spent six months in gaol for attempting to steal morphine from a drug store. Getz was not a pleasant person. Both his marriages failed, the second ending in a long, bitter feud – his wife accused him of domestic violence and he accused her of trying to poison him. Stan was arrogant and temperamental. Famous London jazz club owner Ronnie Scott used to joke that he slipped a disc bending over backwards to please him. Referring to Getz's sudden mood swings, "Zoot" Sims once quipped that he was "a nice bunch of guys".

In 1947, Getz joined "Woody" Herman's Second Herd, a popular and talented band that incorporated elements of bebop into its music. The sax section was particularly strong, featuring Serge Chaloff, "Zoot" Sims and Herbie Steward as well as Stan. They were known as the "four brothers", or, occasionally, "four mothers". Stan's solo on "Early Autumn" made the jazz audience sit up and take notice of his unique sound.

Getz was influenced by Charlie Parker but also by the lighter style of Count Basie's star saxophonist Lester Young. His tone was soft and warm as cashmere. Stan played ballads with sensitivity and intensity but could also swing hard. Saxophonist and critic Greg Fishman has commented that Getz's sound was

> an exquisite combination of light and dark, with a bitter-sweet tinge of sadness. Then there is his taste, which is impeccable: there's an unerring logic to his improvisations. In addition, he has the uncanny ability to play only the essential notes of a phrase. Finesse is something else Getz has in abundance. Every note he plays is a gem: attention is paid to every nuance.

Stan's first significant disc under his own name, *Quartets*, was released in 1950 and immediately became a classic. In 1951, he recorded a live set at the Storyville Club in Boston. Getz plays with great fire but the sound quality is mediocre. More listenable is *Stan Getz Plays* from 1952.

Getz worked with first-rate musicians. On piano successively were Al Haig, Horace Silver, "Duke" Jordan, and Lou Levy. A particular asset in his early groups was the guitar playing of Jimmy Raney, who sounded like "a pupil of Django Reinhardt who developed an admiration for Charlie Parker's music. His tone is cloudy, soft-edged, personal" (Alun Morgan in M Harrison, A Morgan, R Atkins, M James, J Cooke eds, *Modern Jazz, 1945-70: the essential records*, Aquarius Books, 1975). The west coast scene produced a remarkable school of guitarists. As well as Raney (whose son Doug was also an accomplished guitarist), there were Barney Kessel and Herb Ellis (who worked with Charlie Byrd as The Great Guitars), Jim Hall, and Tal Farlow. The last is the least known but one of the best – his technique was so good he was nick-named "the Octopus".

Getz made a triptych of memorable records in the mid-1950s: *West Coast Jazz*, *The Steamer* and *Award Winner*. They featured lengthy, stomping solos from "the Stanley Steamer", as Oscar Peterson dubbed him. There were also, of course, some ravishing ballads. In 1957, Stan made two enjoyable discs with the Peterson trio. The second, *At the Opera House*, is a live recording with master bop trombonist J J Johnson. It features Stan at his most swinging, sounding decidedly Lester Youngish at times.

In 1961, Getz recorded what many consider his masterpiece, *Focus*. It is one of those "with strings" albums that most jazz musicians seem compelled to make at some stage, usually with arrangements that sound like Mantovani. *Focus*, composed and arranged by Eddie Sauter, was different. Sauter, who arranged for Benny Goodman, said in his liner notes:

> I hated the idea of a rhythm section with strings and I also hated the idea of flat backgrounds with no meaning in them-

selves. What I wanted to do was write something like a string quartet, with space to move things. I'd let them make their own time and rhythm. The attack of a rhythm section and strings is different: one is sharp and the other is slow. And they don't blend. I always left in my mind a space for another part to be added. That was the hole I left for Stan. He fitted his part into the fabric and made a whole.

In the 1950s, Brazilian musicians created a synthesis of the traditional samba and cool jazz. After a trip to Rio, guitarist Charlie Byrd was so impressed that he persuaded Getz to join him in recording an album of their compositions. Released in 1962, *Jazz Samba* reached number one in the charts, as did a single from the album, "Desafinado".

In 1963, one of the finest performers in the new Brazilian idiom, singer and guitarist Joao Gilberto, and its best-known composer, Antonio Carlos Jobim, came to New York to record with Getz. The result was another number one hit LP, *Getz/Gilberto*. As the *Penguin Guide to Jazz* aptly observes, it has "hummed seductively around cafes, wine bars and bedrooms for years". There was also a hit single, "The Girl from Ipanema", with a vocal by Joao's wife Astrud. She was not originally supposed to sing but Stan was enthusiastic – he later had an affair with her. The style became known as *bossa nova* and was immensely popular. Almost immediately, record companies had every artist on their books with a heartbeat making a bossa nova LP. For decades, most jazz discs would have at least one number with a Latin beat. Getz rode the crest of the wave in terms of stardom and earnings.

In 1966, Getz made an excellent album with Brazilian guitarist Laurindo Almeida. In response to Almeida's impetus, Getz's playing is "staccato, elegantly fierce and witty. His lean sound varies marvellously in timbre as he spins out the engaging melodies". Almeida was adept at both jazz and classical guitar. In the 1950s, he and altoist "Bud" Shank made a number of recordings of Brazilian music for Pacific Jazz (released on CD as *Brazilliance* vols 1 and 2) that presaged *Jazz Samba* but received little recognition at the time.

In the 1970s, Getz experimented briefly and unsuccessfully with fusion and electronics. In later life, he worked with pianist Kenny Barron and made some interesting records, such as *Anniversary*, recorded live in Copenhagen. However, his playing often lacked its earlier vivacity, and the "beautiful sound", as he once described his tone, had a hollow hoarseness – like a silver plate with deep scratches.

Getz was diagnosed with liver cancer in 1987 and died on 6 June 1991.

18. BENNY GOODMAN (1909-86)

Benjamin David Goodman was born in Chicago on 30 May 1909. His parents were Russian Jewish immigrants and Benny was the ninth of twelve children. They lived in a violent, overcrowded, insanitary slum near the slaughter yards where his father worked as a labourer. David Goodman instilled in his children the imperative to achieve and to improve. He also encouraged them to learn music, particularly as it might bring in some desperately needed dollars. Harry played tuba then string bass and Freddy and Irving became jazz trumpeters. Young Benny was something special – a prodigy who took up the clarinet at age ten and could soon play almost anything. His father parted with some of the family's scarce funds to allow his gifted son to study with a classical clarinet teacher. Although under-age, Benny was soon playing jazz professionally. At 16, he was offered a job by Ben Pollack, one of the most popular white band leaders of the day. In 1929, he joined "Red" Nichols, the doyen of the New York jazz scene.

Benny's sound owed little to the dark, woody style of traditional New Orleans clarinettists such as Johnny Dodds and Barney Bigard. He had a vivid, pure tone, although there was a piquant edge. Goodman's technical ability was close to unlimited – he was comfortable from the chalumeau register up to the highest notes. His solos were flawlessly constructed and his ideas flowed with facility. He could be delicate and lyrical or hot and swinging.

Musically, Benny emerged almost fully formed and just got better. His precocious brilliance meant that he was much in demand as a sideman and he recorded prolifically in his early career. On 22 October 1931, Goodman cut four legendary sides with top New York players Joe Venuti, Eddie Lang and Jack Teagarden: "Beale Street Blues", "After You've Gone", "Farewell Blues", and "Someday Sweetheart". As Dan Morgenstern has said: "There isn't a cut here that fails to swing, and I love his sound from this period, with the grit still in there when he wants it that way. 'Someday Sweetheart' is one of his greatest romantic solos. This man was one hell of a jazz clarinet player".

By 1934, Goodman had formed a big band and featured on the popular radio program Let's Dance. The band was not, however, commercially successful until an engagement at the Palomar Ballroom in Los Angeles in August 1935. Teenage fans descended in multitudes and went wild. Benny recalled:

To our complete amazement, half the crowd stopped dancing and surged around the stand. We finally found people who were up on what we were trying to do. That first big roar from the crowd was the sweetest sound I ever heard in my life – and from that time on the night kept getting bigger and bigger (Ken Burns and Geoffrey Ward, *Jazz: a history of America's music*, Pimlico, 2001).

With a sudden explosion, the Swing era had begun and Benny was its king.

On 3 March 1937, the Goodman band began an engagement at New York's Paramount Theatre. The audience was so enthusiastic that Benny described it as "scary". When the band began playing

despite the best efforts of an army of uniformed ushers to stop them, young people leapt from their seats, filled the aisles, even jumped onto the stage to dance. By three that afternoon, 11,500 teenagers had paid their way inside; by closing time that evening the number had risen to 21,000 and the aisles had been alive with dancers all day (Ken Burns and Geoffrey Ward, *Jazz: a history of America's music*, Pimlico, 2001).

Apart from Goodman, the star soloist was trumpeter Harry James, who was capable of generating tremendous excitement. No-one livened up the rideout to a number like Harry. When Gene Krupa took one of his explosive drum breaks the audiences roared. Goodman pianist Jess Stacy said: "Gene was our salesman, our showman, and he worked hard. You could wring water out of his sleeves when he finished a set". Benny's discipline ensured that the ensemble playing had laser-like precision. He also employed excellent vocalists such as Helen Ward and Martha Tilton. A collection of radio broadcasts from 1937-38, *On the Air*, shows just how good the band was and why the "bobby soxers" mobbed Benny.

Part of Goodman's success was due to Fletcher Henderson's arrangements, which gave him more punch than the average white dance band. Henderson's orchestra was one of the most influential in the US for a decade but he was not cut out to be a leader and by now was down on his luck. As well as providing some much needed cash, Benny gave Henderson full credit for his work. The band's book was also augmented by charts from other top arrangers such as Jimmy Mundy and Edgar Sampson.

Goodman was highly disciplined and determined. A perfectionist, he was intolerant of inferior performance from himself or anyone else. At times arrogant, abrasive and insensitive, Benny was not easy to work with. He had a killing look known as "the ray" that he would focus on those who displeased him. The band was run on militaristic lines with no allowance for human frailty. Helen Ward, who was in love with Benny, told the story of rehearsing with him on a bitter winter day. When she complained that it was cold, Benny agreed and went and got himself a sweater.

The Goodman band reached its apogee at a concert at Carnegie Hall on 16 January 1938. Benny was apprehensive as it was the first time jazz had been played in those august walls. It was a sell-out and became his most famous recording. If I had to name a single jazz performance as my favourite, this would be it.

Proceedings livened up with "Honeysuckle Rose", a jam with members of the Basie and Ellington bands. The array of soloists is mouth-watering: the Count and colleagues Lester Young and "Buck" Clayton; Ellingtonians Johnny Hodges and Harry Carney; Harry James and Goodman. The rhythm section defined the term: Basie's Walter Page and Freddie Green plus Krupa. The excitement grew and grew. It culminated in "Sing, Sing, Sing". Classical and jazz critic Irving Kolodin, who was involved with the organisation of the concert, wrote: "With the end of a hectic evening in sight and no lingering concerns about the success of the program, the band seems to be playing at last for its own pleasure only, with rather remarkable results". Benny hits high C at the end of his solo. Next comes a surprising interlude from pianist Jess Stacy. He had been listening to Debussy that morning and decided to lower the temperature with an introspective, impressionistic solo. Benny approved, moving the microphone closer as Stacy played. Krupa then thunders in and the number comes to a scorching climax. Many years ago, I played "Sing, Sing, Sing" to a fellow student who was driving cabs part-time. He made a cassette recording of it (as one did in those primitive days) and played it when he was driving. He told me that just about every passenger that night said: what's that music? It's fantastic. If you don't enjoy this one, maybe you should be playing croquet instead.

By the 1940s, some of the spark had gone out of the Goodman band. It sounded less spontaneous and more formulaic. James and Krupa had both departed. There were still some fine moments, however, such as "Clarinet a la King", a mini concerto for Benny written and arranged by Eddie Sauter. "Stealin' Apples", recorded live in 1943 at the Hotel Astor in New York, has one of Benny's most perfect solos.

As significant as Benny's big band were his small groups – some would say more so. Jazz writer Richard Sudhalter has commented:

> In common with other virtuosi, Benny Goodman often seemed more comfortable making music with intimate, even informal, small groups. Not that the frisson – the sheer voltage – of full band performances lacked its vivid seductions, rather the chamber setting elicited refinements, a full play of colour and dynamics, a spontaneous interplay and subtlety of phrase, that are triumphs of Goodman's work.

John Hammond, Long Island patrician, jazz promoter, and relentless self-promoter, was a friend of Benny's and later his brother-in-law. The two were eventually to fall out due to Hammond's propensity to interfere and criticise. One of his better ideas was the Goodman trio. Benny had been very taken with the work of pianist Teddy Wilson, who was classically trained and also a perfectionist. The two were interested in recording together and Hammond set up a session in July 1935. Gene Krupa was the third participant. Teddy played long, graceful lines with clarity and precision, blending perfectly with Goodman. The next year, vibraphonist Lionel Hampton made it a quartet. In later years, Hamp's unrelenting exuberance could be irritating but at this stage he added a touch of zest without being overbearing. The effect of Lionel's glistening vibes on "Moonglow", his first recording with the quartet, is magical. Hamp and Teddy were never members of the big band, but quartet and trio performances were a regular part of concerts. The fact that Wilson and Hampton were black caused consternation but Goodman was more concerned with a musician's ability than their colour: "If a guy's got it, let him give it. I'm selling music, not prejudice". It was a major milestone in making mixed race bands publicly acceptable.

Between 1937 and 1939, Benny cut 47 trio and quartet tracks for RCA. All are examples of swinging, supremely inventive jazz. In 1947, he recorded a further flawless trio session with Teddy Wilson. He returned to the format in 1954 with Jimmy Rowles and then Mel Powell on piano. Almost as good as the 1930s sides, these later sessions have been re-issued on CD as *The Complete Capitol Trios*. A re-union with Wilson, Hampton and Krupa in 1964, *Together Again*, was a highlight of Goodman's later output. On "Four Once More", the quartet plays with as much fire and enthusiasm as it ever did.

In 1939 Goodman formed a sextet featuring pioneering electric guitarist Charlie Christian. After Christian's untimely death in 1942, Goodman continued to record with a sextet, often drawing on members of the big band. At one stage, trombonist Lou McGarity featured in the front line and the combination of clarinet and trombone worked well. On piano at various times were Teddy Wilson, Fletcher Henderson, Count Basie and Mel Powell, and on vibes Lionel Hampton, Red Norvo and Terry Gibbs. When the big bands went out of fashion in the 1950s, Benny worked solely with small ensembles. The later sextet recordings are not well known but are delightful listening.

As the market for mainstream jazz revived, Benny regularly reformed the big band, toured and recorded. With his unerring ear, he recruited the cream of new talent. In 1962, Goodman made a ground-breaking tour of the USSR. After the trip it was said that "the swing music that had once set the jitterbugs dancing in the Paramount aisles almost blew down the Iron Curtain".

Goodman took an increasing interest in classical music. In 1938, he recorded Mozart's clarinet quintet with the celebrated Budapest Quartet. *The Penguin Guide to Recorded Classical Music* (8th ed) gives the CD version a top rating, describing it as a stylish performance, adding waspishly: "These were the days when popular musicians were musically educated". In the 1940s, Benny studied with classical clarinettist Reginald Kell, re-learning his technique. He recorded Mozart's clarinet concerto and those of Weber and Nielsen. Goodman premiered Bartok's *Contrasts* and Poulenc's clarinet sonata. Malcolm Arnold, Aaron Copland, Paul Hindemith and Darius Milhaud wrote concertos for him. The Copland has become a standard work in the classical repertoire.

Benny Goodman died of a heart attack on 13 June 1986. He left a considerable estate: frugality and prudent financial management had made him a rich man. Jazz promoter George Wein summed up the Goodman legacy: "He proved that good music could reach the general public. He was the most popular figure in the history of jazz to reach a non-jazz public. He was the Beatles of his day. And he did it with pure, uncompromising music. He never compromised" (*New York Times*, 14 June 1986).

19. DEXTER GORDON (1923-1990)

Dexter Keith Gordon was born on 27 February 1923 in Los Angeles. His father was that relatively rare thing in the US at the time, a black medical practitioner. Dexter was a child prodigy and was playing tenor saxophone professionally in his teens. He worked with Lionel Hampton in the early 1940s, then did a spell with Billy Eckstine's band.

There was a flourishing post-war jazz scene in Los Angeles. Dex and fellow bop tenor pioneer, Wardell Gray, were a popular double, engaging in long duels. These became famous on record as "The Chase" and "The Steeplechase". Gray was a heroin addict and in 1955 his body was found dumped in the desert outside Las Vegas.

He had a broken neck – how he acquired it has never been satis-factorily explained. Dexter was also addicted and an alcoholic. He spent much of the 1950s in and out of gaol, although by the next decade had his demons under some sort of control.

Gordon had a gruff but emotive sound. His solos consisted of long, flowing lines that seemed as though they would go on forever. Dex could play with the rushing urgency of a tsunami or wring every last drop out of a ballad. Jazz writer Robert Palmer has said that Gordon's sound was "huge and encompassing, from his booming lower register all the way up to a rich falsetto range. He was a master of harmonic subtleties and a master of timing. He was a prankster who enjoyed inserting little musical jokes. Above all, he was an architect of sound. His choruses have an ineluctable certainty to them". Dexter influenced Sonny Rollins and John Coltrane. In turn, their advances fed back into his style.

In May 1961, Alfred Lion of Blue Note records enticed Gordon to New York to make two classic albums, *Doin' Allright* which featured trumpeter Freddie Hubbard, and *Dexter Calling*, a quartet record. Against the tide of critical opinion, I prefer the latter as I find the playing of Hubbard brash and obtrusive at times. Further celebrated records for Blue Note followed. The pick of them are *Go!* and *Our Man In Paris*, which features "Bud" Powell on piano. Although advanced in his sad decline, Powell staged a rare return to form on this occasion.

In 1963, Dexter moved to Europe. He recorded prolifically, indeed indiscriminately, for the Danish Steeplechase label. Like many black jazz musicians, Gordon found life in Europe more congenial than in the racist USA. From the late 1960s, Gordon travelled periodically to the States to record for Prestige. His first LP for that label was appropriately called *Tower of Power*. My favourite disc from this series is *The Panther* (1970), with that consummately tasteful pianist, Tommy Flanagan. A good sampler of Dexter's work from this period is *The Art of the Ballad* (1969-73, released 1998).

In 1976, Dex returned to New York for a triumphant engagement at the Village Vanguard. The queues were round the block. According to Robert Palmer, Charlie Mingus spent an afternoon listening to Gordon, "urging the saxophonist on with shouts and laughter. 'Yeah, yeah', he would exclaim when Gordon played a particularly felicitous phrase, 'You're gonna be teaching New York some stuff, man. Some lessons.'" The Vanguard engagement is documented on a live recording, *Homecoming*. I can still remember hearing a track on an ABC jazz program when it was first released. It was one of those "I've got to listen until the end to find out who this is" moments. I rushed out the next day and bought the LP and have been a Gordon fan ever since. Another good record from that time, less raucous than the Vanguard date, is *Biting the Apple*, with Barry Harris on piano. Gordon had discriminating taste in pianists – as well as Flanagan and Harris, he worked with Kenny Drew, Hamp Hawes, Wyn Kelly and George Cables. In 1977, Gordon resettled permanently in the US.

"Long Tall Dexter" was six foot five, handsome and charismatic, with a resonant baritone voice. He was a natural for the stage and acting was his other career. In 1960, he featured in Jack Gelber's play about heroin addiction, *The Connection*. Gordon shot to fame when he portrayed an ageing, down-on-his-luck jazz musician in Bertrand Tavernier's 1987 film *'Round Midnight*. His character, Dale Turner, was a combination of Lester Young, "Bud" Powell and himself. Gordon was nominated for an Academy Award for Best Actor. Just before his death he filmed Awakenings with Robert de Niro.

Suffering from emphysema, Gordon did not play much in the 1980s. He died of kidney failure and cancer of the larynx on 25 April 1990. He is said to have been surprised that he lasted so long.

20. HAMPTON HAWES (1928-77)

Hampton Barnett Hawes was one of the best pianists of the bebop generation, but drug addiction blighted his career and he remains undeservedly neglected. Hamp was born in Los Angeles on 13 November 1928. His father was a Presbyterian clergyman and his mother played piano at services. She taught Hamp to play at an early age. He had little other tuition but soaked up the gospel music and spirituals in his father's church. As a nine-year-old, Hawes stopped going to church on Sunday with the rest of the family and secretly, as his father considered jazz sinful on the Sabbath, played boogie woogie on the upright at home: "The piano was the only sure friend I had because it was the only thing that was consistent, always made sense and responded directly to what I did. The piano was the first secure and honest thing in my life. I could approach it on my own and fail or be good" (Hampton Hawes with Don Asher, *Raise up off Me: a portrait of Hampton Hawes*, Coward, McCann and Geoghegan, 1974).

As a teenager, Hamp worked with many of the top west coast musicians, such as Dexter Gordon, Wardell Gray and Art Pepper. He played in trumpeter Howard "Maggie" McGhee's band with the father of bebop, altoist Charlie Parker. Like all of them, Hawes became a heroin addict. His time in the Army during the Korean War was a litany of disciplinary proceedings caused by his habit.

Critic Alun Morgan has encapsulated the key elements of Hawes' style:

> His playing has been described as a literal keyboard transcription of Charlie Parker; certainly it is more like Parker than, say, 'Bud' Powell, and Hawes claimed Powell never was a direct influence. Like Parker again Hawes has a great gift for playing the blues. Fast tempos give Hawes few problems, and he has no difficulty in maintaining the logic and continuity of this thoughts while playing at around 80 bars to the minute. On the other hand he can produce out of tempo performances which have considerable beauty and charm. In later years jazz was plagued with 'soul' and 'funky' pianists, none of whom had anything approaching Hawes' understanding of the blues idiom. He was head and shoulders above his competitors (M Harrison, A Morgan, R Atkins, M James, J Cooke eds, *Modern Jazz, 1945-70: the essential records*, Aquarius Books, 1975).

Hamp formed a trio with bassist "Red" Mitchell and drummer Chuck Thompson. In 1955, they made three of the finest piano jazz albums ever recorded, *The Trio*, *This Is Hampton Hawes*, and *Ev-*

erybody Likes Hampton Hawes. The following year Hamp recorded *All Night Session*, released on three CDs, with a quartet including guitarist Jim Hall. Another worthwhile recording from this period is *Four*, with the all-star rhythm section of Barney Kessel, Red Mitchell and Shelly Manne. *The Sermon*, recorded in 1958 but not released until 1987, has Hamp drawing on his gospel roots.

These should have been good year for Hawes. He was musically at his peak and was gaining critical and popular recognition. Unfortunately, his out of control heroin habit was undermining his health and success. After a 1957 tour finishing in Washington, Hawes was so broke that he couldn't pay his hotel bill and left all his clothes behind. He arrived back in New York in bad shape:

> Fifty cents in my pocket, no clothes and no job, but a thin line to various brothers around town. Standing under a streetlight at 45th and Broadway when a brother walks up to me. 'Hamp, what're you doin'?' 'Nothin' I focus and see it's Charles Mingus. 'Man, I wish you could get yourself together, you got too much talent to go down the drain. I ought to call your father. You need some money?' 'Shit, yes'. 'I've got a record date for a trio this weekend. You got it if you can get yourself together'. 'Would you care to give me a retainer?' 'Damn, Hamp, you won't even spare me' (Hampton Hawes with Don Asher, *Raise up off Me: a portrait of Hampton Hawes*, Coward, McCann and Geoghegan, 1974).

Mingus came up with the cash and Hawes immediately used it to shoot up. Considering the circumstances, he played amazingly well on the day.

In 1958, Hamp was arrested for drug offences. Poet and novelist Ishmael Reed wrote this account of Hawes' downfall and redemption:

When I lived in New York during the early 1960s, John F Kennedy was a hero among the downtown art crowd — not because of any legislative or foreign policy achievement, but because he pardoned the jazz pianist Hampton Hawes. Hawes was a bebop pianist with a right hand technique so brilliant that he was admired by none other than Art Tatum, widely considered the greatest jazz pianist ever. Hawes had been sentenced to ten years in a Fort Worth prison for buying drugs from an undercover agent. 'Just after my third Christmas I was watching John Kennedy accept the Presidency on the Washington steps', Hawes wrote later. 'Something about him, the voice, the eyes, the way he stood bright and coatless and proud in that cold air. I thought, that's the right cat; looks like he got some soul and might listen'. He applied for a pardon, and received one from the President on 16 August 1963 (*New York Times*, 18 December 2013).

In 1964, Hawes made *The Green Leaves of Summer*, a joyful record that has the feel of a man celebrating his freedom. His career revived only fitfully after his release. Although there is some fine pianism on his later recordings, he never regained the sustained brilliance of his early work. Hamp spent his best years high or in gaol. An attempt to regain popularity in the 1970s through electronics and fusion was a dismal failure.

Hawes' frank, at times harrowing, autobiography, *Raise Up off Me*, written with musician and author Don Asher, was published in 1974. As well as giving insights into the pioneers of bebop, it documents graphically the self-destruction and degradation of the life of a heroin addict (*Raise up off Me: a portrait of Hampton Hawes*, Coward, McCann and Geoghegan, 1974). Hampton Hawes died of a massive stroke on 22 May 1977 at the age of 48.

22. COLEMAN HAWKINS (1904-69)

It is hard to imagine jazz without the tenor saxophone, yet it was invented as a jazz instrument in the 1920s by Coleman Hawkins:

There were saxophonists in jazz bands before Hawkins began to develop his manner of playing in the mid-1920s. But they were using a slap-tongue effect, which resulted in a chicken-like sound, reflecting the prevalent feeling that the saxophone was essentially a comic instrument. Hawkins used a big tone and a heavy vibrato. His swaggering attack drove along relentlessly through intensely rhythmic, choppy phrases (John S Wilson, *New York Times*, 20 May 1969).

Almost all major tenor players were influenced by Hawkins: Ben Webster, Don Byas, "Buddy" Tate, Paul Gonsalves, and later giants such as "Sonny" Rollins and John Coltrane. Lester Young, his main stylistic rival, acknowledged a significant debt.

Coleman Randolph Hawkins was born in Missouri on 21 November 1904. His mother was an amateur musician who ensured he was musically well-educated. He also studied music at high school and college in Kansas. Taking up tenor sax at nine, Hawkins was working professionally by the age of 14. He first came to prominence when he joined the Fletcher Henderson Orchestra in 1924.

Henderson was a pioneering big band leader and arranger who paved the way for the Swing era. Benny Carter, who was with Henderson in the early 1930s, said it was the outfit that "everybody was hoping to play with – it was the acid test. If you could make it with Fletcher you could make it with anybody. It was the hardest music and the best music around". Hawkins put it more simply: "It was a stompin' band, yeah man".

A particular strength of the Henderson orchestra was its stellar array of soloists, starting with Louis Armstrong. Others in the trumpet chair at various times were Rex Stewart, Roy Eldridge, and Henry "Red" Allen", after Louis the greatest trumpeter to come out of New Orleans. Also in the brass section were trombonists Benny Morton and JC Higginbotham. On reeds, as well as Carter and Hawkins, were Russell Procope, Don Redman, and the excellent clarinettist "Buster" Bailey.

In his decade with Henderson, Hawkins established himself as the king of the tenor sax. He had a powerful, roaring sound and chugged through up-tempo numbers like a steam train. Hawk's tone could be as grainy as sandpaper, yet he played ballads with intimacy and emotion. There was a dark grandeur to his music, like a mountain range at sunset.

Hawkins made the most of his celebrity. According to jazz writer Al Van Starrex, he "lived and dressed in style, driving the fastest cars, consuming legendary quantities of food and liquor, but never bragging". He didn't have to given his obvious mastery of his instrument. Personally, Hawk was a reserved loner who had little in life other than music. He was fiercely competitive, delighting in "cutting competitions" where he consistently put all comers in their place.

In 1934, Hawkins went to London to join Jack Hylton's dance band. Soon after, the band embarked on a tour of Europe, including Germany. When the Nazis objected to Hawkins' presence because of his colour, Hylton proceeded on without him. He has been criticised for this but jazz scholar and musician Tony Baldwin has put it in perspective:

> With the intransigence of the Nazi authorities, and German venues doubtless already sold-out, there weren't many real grounds for Hylton to call off the tour, whatever we might think now. It's also worth remembering that it didn't stop him taking several Jewish bandsmen to Berlin, including Freddy Schweitzer, who was German and so presumably unemployable in his own country. As Hylton had already postponed the German tour for a fortnight, my hunch is that the problems with Hawkins' German entry permit began before the band left London. Perhaps this breather gave Hylton's office time to set up substitute gigs for Hawkins with the Ramblers in Holland, because, after all, Hylton was Hawk's European agent (email to the author).

Freed of Hylton's staid orchestra, Hawkins spent five productive years in Europe where he was received with enthusiasm. In terms of recording, the high point was a session in Paris on 28 April 1937 with fellow Henderson alumnus Benny Carter and the cream of local musicians, including the phenomenal Gypsy guitarist "Django" Reinhardt, and Stephane Grappelli, on this occasion playing piano rather than violin. As well as high voltage versions of "Honeysuckle Rose", "Crazy Rhythm" and "Sweet Georgia Brown", the band recorded a rhapsodic "Out of Nowhere".

Hawkins arrived back in New York in 1939. Tenor players who had come to prominence in his absence, or thought they had, were eager to take him on. In a series of duels at after-hours clubs frequented by musicians Hawk carved them all. One of the vanquished said: "Well that's that. Coleman's still the boss, and when you tangle with him you'd better know what you are doing or you better ask someone" (Ken Burns and Geoffrey Ward, *Jazz: a history of America's music*, Pimlico, 2001).

In October 1939, Hawkins recorded "Body and Soul". It was an unexpected best-seller which has become synonymous with him. Hawk's solo has the ornate opulence of a Venetian palazzo. He starts soft and breathy, then pours out chorus after sublime chorus as the tension builds to an epic conclusion.

The 1940s was the era of bebop, which many earlier players disparaged. Louis Armstrong described it as "Chinese music". Hawkins, however, welcomed the new style, although his basic approach did not change. He jammed with many of the original boppers and hired the then extremely iconoclastic pianist Thelonious Monk. In 1957, Monk returned the favour and asked Hawk to play on his classic *Monk's Music* LP. The elder statesman handled Monk's complex music with aplomb.

The 1950s was a quiet time for Swing era players such as Hawkins. Late in the decade, realising there was a nostalgia market, record companies began to get them back into the studio. These LPs appealed, as well, to jazz fans who found bop uncongenial. In 1957, Hawkins bounced back with *The Hawk Flies High*, which matched him with two boppers, J J Johnson on trombone and trumpeter Idrees Sulieman. He cut two excellent LPs for Verve in the same year, *The Genius of Coleman Hawkins* and *Encounters Ben Webster*. In 1958 came *The High and Mighty Hawk* – speaks for itself really.

Hawkins next signed with Prestige, and more classic records resulted. Highlights include pairings with two master pianists, *At Ease* with Tommy Flanagan and *With the Red Garland Trio*. In 1961, *The Hawk Relaxes* was released. By now, he was starting to sound a mite too relaxed but this is a very enjoyable set of typically lyrical ballad performances. A session with "Duke" Ellington the next year challenged Hawkins into some of his finest playing.

Hawkins went into a sad decline as the 1960s progressed. Van Starrex comments: "By 1969 the Hawk was a shell of his old magisterial self, a frail bearded figure wracked by alcohol and starvation. He could barely hold his horn and was liable to collapse on stage – although he continued to produce majestic music". Coleman Hawkins died of liver disease on 19 May 1969.

22. BILLIE HOLIDAY (1915-59)

The 1930s was the era of the great jazz singers. Benny Goodman featured Helen Ward and later Peggy Lee, Helen Forrest sang with Artie Shaw, Helen Humes belted out the blues for Count Basie, Ella Fitzgerald came to prominence with "Chick" Webb before making her famous songbook albums in the 1950s. The greatest, most original singer of the Swing era was Billie Holiday. Born on 7 April 1915, Billie was brought up as **Eleanora Fagan**, the illegitimate child of Sarah Fagan and jazz musician Clarence Holiday, who quickly disappeared from the scene. After a childhood of upheaval and poverty, Billie became a prostitute at age 12. In 1929, she was gaoled when the brothel she was working in was raided.

The legacy of Billie's appalling early life was compounded by her headstrong, at times uncontrollable, personality. A night club owner said:

> She did what she liked. If a man came up she liked, she'd go with him; if a woman, the same thing. If she was handed a drink, she'd drink it. If you had a stick of pot, she'd take a cab ride on her break and smoke it. If you had something stronger she'd use that. When she told you off, you were damn well told – white, black, rich, poor (Ken Burns and Geoffrey Ward, *Jazz: a history of America's music*, Pimlico, 2001).

Throughout her life Billie had a series of disastrous relationships with often abusive partners.

Billie made use of her vocal talent to sing for tips in small New York clubs. Her influences were Bessie Smith and Louis Armstrong. In 1933, jazz producer and entrepreneur John Hammond heard her and was hugely impressed, particularly by the fact that she used her voice to improvise like an instrument. Billie made up for her limited range by the phrasing and expressiveness of her singing and her sombre, gravelly tone. Even on an upbeat number, there is a sadness underlying her music. When she sings, in "Some Other Spring", "Sunshine's all around me but deep in my heart it's cold as ice" you can feel the chill. And never play "Gloomy Sunday" on a Sunday morning with a hangover or you will feel ten times worse.

In 1935, Hammond arranged for Billie to record with a hand-picked small group, including Benny Goodman, Ben Webster and "Buck" Clayton, and her career was launched. She went on to make more than 300 records for Columbia in the next nine years, many produced by Hammond. The best of them feature the filigreed piano of Teddy Wilson and the beguiling tone of Billie's close friend, tenor saxophonist Lester Young. They are her enduring legacy and definitive small group jazz. Critic Gary Giddins has said:

> These exemplary tracks overflow with detail and invention, rarely wasting a second, with each player obliged to make a personal, identifiable statement in just a few measures. Hammond raided the big bands that happened to be playing in New York when a session was scheduled, recruiting key players from Basie, Ellington, Goodman, Calloway, and the rest. These sessions remain an unbeatable primer on the leading soloists and rhythm players of the swing era.

In April 1939 Billie recorded her most famous song, "Strange Fruit", with starkly confronting lyrics about lynchings, which, even at that time, were still taking place in Dear Old Dixie.

Billie had a brief, less than successful, period as a big band singer. She worked with Count Basie in 1937 until they fell out and he fired her. A regrettably small number of recordings document the partnership. "They Can't Take That Away from Me", recorded live at the Savoy Ballroom, is Billie at her relaxed, swinging peak. It has an intensity lacking in the studio version. In 1938, Artie Shaw invited Billie to join his band, an extremely controversial move in the segregated USA of the day. She quit after nine months, unable to endure the racial humiliations and degradations: staying in different hotels to white members of the band, having to use the service elevator at the Lincoln Hotel in New York, unable to sing on radio broadcasts because she sounded too black. Billie recorded just one track with Shaw, "Any Old Time" – a masterpiece that showcases both at their best.

By the 1940s, Billie was a commercial and critical success. However, drug and alcohol abuse impeded her career. In 1947, she was imprisoned for possession of narcotics. Her fame, perhaps more accurately notoriety, was enhanced by her frank 1956 autobiography, *Lady Sings the Blues*, ghosted by journalist William Dufty. In 1972, it formed the basis of a movie starring Diana Ross. As the 1950s progressed, Billie became increasingly erratic and unreliable and her singing deteriorated noticeably. Listening to her last recordings is a painful experience – the voice is like the stump of a broken tooth.

Billie Holiday died of cirrhosis of the liver on 17 July 1959. She was arrested in her hospital room for drug offences just before her death.

"ILLINOIS" JACQUET (1922-2004)

The original stompin', hollerin', honkin' tenor man was "Illinois" Jacquet. Lester Young was an influence, as was Ben Webster, particularly in his ballad playing. Rhythm and blues was a strong inspiration – Jacquet would have been at home in BB King's band. He was also a proficient vocalist in the "blues shouter" tradition.

In his day, Jacquet was one of the most exciting players in jazz, regularly whipping audiences into a frenzy. An accomplished showman, Jacquet's suit would often be sodden with perspiration when he left the stage. While this aspect of his playing led to early recognition, it also stereotyped him for life, obscuring his genuine talent.

Ill-disposed critics dubbed him "Ill-noise". The *Penguin Guide to Jazz* (6th ed) has perceptively observed that Jacquet had

> a big, blues tone edged with a kind of desperate loneliness that somehow underlines his status as a permanent guest star, an unbreakable mustang of a player who was never given the right amount of room or genuinely sympathetic sidemen. His playing can show remarkable sensitivity and he is one of the fastest thinkers in the business.

Jean-Baptiste Jacquet was born in Louisiana on 30 October 1922 and grew up in Houston, Texas. He said that his nickname came from "Illinwek, which is an Indian word for superior man. I don't know how I came to deserve that!" At age three, he was tap dancing in a family band led by his father. When he was 15, he was working with local jazz groups. Jacquet's big break came when, as a 19-year-old, he played a famous solo with Lionel Hampton's band on "Flying Home". He subsequently worked with "Cab" Calloway and "Count" Basie. Another classic early Jacquet solo was on Basie's "The King" from 1946.

From the 1940s, Jacquet became a regular with Norman Granz's popular Jazz at the Philharmonic concerts. They were basically jam sessions featuring a sometimes ill-assorted agglomeration of stars. Jacquet's role was to bring the audience to its feet with his galvanising solos. His technique was to contrast high notes not usually heard on the tenor with repeated growling, gritty low register phrases. Critic Roy Carr has commented that the "screams and scrambles, the honks and hysteria, are not far removed from the sounds of the free jazz movement two decades in the future".

Consistency was Jacquet's strength during his long career. Unlike his youthful colleague Dexter Gordon, he never progressed much stylistically – although the solos became less frenetic and more magisterial – but listeners knew what they were getting and enjoyed it. Jacquet commented: "Jazz is deeper than people think. It is a spiritual form of art. It's like a Picasso painting. There's no such thing as art going out of style" (*Washington Post*, 24 July 2004).

An excellent survey of Jacquet's output in the 1950s is *Flying Home: the best of the Verve Years*. Later highlights are *The Message* (1963), on which he solos effectively on bassoon, *The Blues, That's Me* (1969), and *God Bless My Solo* (1978). The hard swinging *Live at Schaffhausen*, recorded in 1978 with another evergreen, Hank Jones, shows just how exciting Jacquet could still be in concert.

In 1993 Jacquet's band performed at President Bill Clinton's inaugural ball. A long-time fan, Clinton borrowed Jacquet's saxophone to play a solo. Jacquet was still performing regularly in his 80s. He died of a heart attack on 22 July 2004.

24. KEITH JARRETT (1945-)

Keith Jarrett is egotistical, self-indulgent, temperamental – and undoubtedly a genius. He is the most significant jazz pianist since Bill Evans and one of the greatest ever. When some thought jazz was dead, and many practitioners lent credence to the theory with meaningless electronic noodling, Jarrett resuscitated acoustic piano, the trio, and the music. He broke through improvisatory barriers by integrating long impressionistic passages into his solos. Jarrett empowered and inspired a new generation of jazz pianists such as Brad Mehldau and Fred Hersch.

Jarrett's virtuosity is extraordinary. Stylistically, he ranges effortlessly across mainstream jazz, free form, minimalism, experimentalism and classical music. He is also a talented multi-instrumentalist. After hearing Jarrett play guitar in a club, Stan Getz offered him a job!

The *Penguin Guide to Jazz* (8th ed) has accurately observed: "Jarrett divides critical opinion widely. The sheer momentum of early success has allowed him to experiment freely, but it has also allowed an unusual and not always desirable licence to experiment in public and to release a prodigious number of records". During his career, he has been "maddeningly indulgent and selflessly brilliant by turns". Jarrett does seem to suffer from the conviction that every note he has ever recorded is worthy of release.

Keith Jarrett was born in Allentown, Pennsylvania on 8 May 1945. Contrary to a widely held belief, he is not Afro-American, having European ancestry on both his father and mother's side. Ornette Coleman, after listening to Jarrett play, once came up to him and said: "Man, you have to be black!" Jarrett replied: "I know. I'm working on it".

A true prodigy, Jarrett began playing piano at three and gave his first public recital at seven. He studied classical music throughout his childhood and was briefly a student at Berklee College of Music. In 1964, he moved to New York to play jazz. Jarrett's ability meant that he was not short of work. Art Blakey asked Jarrett to join the Jazz Messengers, after which he worked with tenor saxophonist Charles Lloyd's fusion quartet. From 1970-71, Jarrett was with Miles Davis, playing electric piano and organ. In the early 1970s he began working as a leader, forming a quartet with bassist Charlie Haden, drummer Paul Motian and tenor saxophonist Dewey Redman. He also had a European quartet featuring Jan Garbarek on tenor. In addition, Jarrett made a number of recordings of his orchestral compositions and others where he played every instrument – proficiently, of course.

After his time with Miles, Jarrett rejected electronics, stating that the electricity should come from the music. At about this time, German producer Manfred Eicher invited him to record for his new ECM label. Liking the freedom Eicher offered and the sound he obtained, Jarrett agreed. The association continued throughout his career. Jarrett has said:

> If I hadn't found Manfred Eicher there would be no solo albums. I would have a desk full of scores that had never been rehearsed, not to mention played or recorded. I'm working on the music and Manfred on his sound. When he puts the recording on he wants to hear what he heard when it was happening.

With Eicher's encouragement, Jarrett began to perform totally improvised solo piano concerts, an astonishing concept then as now. He has said that neither he nor Eicher had any idea of how successful they would be. In 1975, *The Koln Concert* was released, Jarrett's most famous disc and the best-selling piano record of all time. It is almost Lisztian in its drama, lyricism and colour. Quiet passages slowly build into intense climaxes. The work has a wholeness and structure lacking in some of his other solo recitals. The cherry on the cake is an astonishingly beautiful encore, with a melody as catchy as any Top 40 hit.

Throughout his career, Jarrett has regularly returned to solo concerts. Given the nature of the high wire act he is undertaking, it doesn't always work. Nonetheless, most of his solo recordings have some memorable moments. Jarrett has nominated *Vienna* (1991) as a personal favourite. *La Scala* (1997) is a memorable achievement.

A 2005 recital at Carnegie Hall marked a new direction. Without the symphonic grandeur (sometimes grandiosity) of earlier performances, it was divided into shorter pieces – more Debussy than Liszt. A drawback is that, in typical Jarrett fashion, the prolonged adulatory applause between each item is retained in its entirety, making it difficult listening.

Of solo improvisation, Jarrett has said:

> The first answer to the question how do I create is 'I don't know'. I think that's an important part of the answer, and it may be the most important part. When I play pure improvisation, any kind of intellectual and emotional handles are inappropriate to just letting the river move where it's supposed to move. If you are a rock climber, once you are halfway up the space of a cliff, you have to keep moving, you have to keep going somewhere. And that's what I do. The best improvisations I know of are made when you have no ideas.

The intense concentration needed to improvise has made Jarrett notoriously intolerant of badly behaved audiences – well, that's his story, anyway. In 2007, when he came on stage at the Umbria Jazz Festival and saw people at the front taking photos, he stormed to the microphone and abused "all these assholes with cameras. Turn them f...ing off right now. If we see any more lights I reserve the right – and I think the privilege is yours to hear us – but I reserve the right to stop playing and leave the god-damn city" (*JazzTimes*, 15 July 2013).

In 1999, Jarrett made a very different solo record, *The Melody at Night with You*. Dedicated to his then wife Rose Anne, it consists of delicate versions of standard tunes. A reunion in 2007 with bassist Charlie Haden resulted in *Jasmine*. Recorded at Jarrett's home studio, a converted barn on his property in rural New Jersey, it features subtle but beautiful versions of standards. Haden's mellow, woody bass blends perfectly with Jarrett's playing. A second volume, *Last Dance*, was released in 2014. In his liner notes to Jasmine, Jarrett says: "Call your wife or husband or lover in late at night and sit down and listen. These are great love songs played by players who are trying, mostly, to keep the message intact. I hope you can hear it the way we did".

In 1983, Jarrett teamed up with bassist Gary Peacock and drummer Jack DeJohnette in what became known as the Standards Trio, the repertoire being drawn mainly from the "great American songbook". It was like the Bill Evans trio modernised. All members had considerable independence but worked interdependently. Jarrett's playing incorporated the freedom that he pioneered with his solo concerts but is anchored by the bass and drums. The trio usually kept within the bounds of traditional jazz performance. At its best, it is a very rewarding mix.

Standards Volume One and Volume Two were recorded at the same session in January 1983. Both are excellent records, though *Volume One* is marred by a God-awful version of "God Bless the Child", which is transmogrified into a quarter of an hour of rhythmically repetitive droning. Such episodes are a jarring feature of Jarrett's work, like a recurrent nervous tic. *Bye Bye Blackbird*, for example, a tribute to Miles Davis, features some of Jarrett's best bebop playing. Unfortunately, it also has "For Miles", almost 20 minutes of directionless, low register chording to a monotonous beat. Did he really like Miles?

The Standards Trio has mainly recorded in concert. *Standards Live*, recorded in Paris in 1985, maintained the elevated level of the initial studio recordings. *Still Live* from the following year has some high spots but is less focussed overall. *The Cure*, from a New York concert in 1990, is more consistently satisfying. One of Jarrett's most enjoyable trio records (with Paul Motian on drums rather than DeJohnette) is *At the Deer Head Inn*, recorded in 1992 at a venue in his hometown where he had his first serious job as a jazz musician. He has rightly commented: "I think that you can hear on this tape what jazz is all about".

An engagement at the Blue Note in 1994 yielded a six CD set. The *Penguin Guide* observes: "It might be considered 'warts and all' but for the fact that there are no warts. Nor is there any repetition or aimless noodling … As an insight into how spontaneously creative Jarrett can be it is unparalleled" – well, relatively few blemishes anyway. Other enjoyable trio recordings are *Yesterdays, Standards in Norway, Tokyo '96* and *Whisper Not*.

Classical performance has been a feature of Jarrett's career. He has recorded keyboard works by Bach and Handel, Mozart piano concertos, and Shostakovich's *Twenty Four Preludes and Fugues*. To celebrate Jarrett's 70th birthday in 2015, ECM released a recording he made in the mid-1980s of piano concertos by Samuel Barber and Bela Bartok. A review in the British classical music bible *Gramophone* said: "Although many jazz pianists unquestionably play classical music well, do their performances stack up to those of world-class, full-time classical keyboard practitioners? In the case of these live archival Barber and Bartok Third Concertos with Keith Jarrett, the answer is an unequivocal yes" (Issue No. 7, 2015).

In 2018, Jarrett suffered two major strokes and retired from performing. His gargantuan output sprawls massively but unevenly across the jazz landscape.

25. HANK JONES (1918-2020)

Sophistication, good taste and lyricism were the hallmarks of Hank Jones' pianism. He had perfect execution, inventiveness, and an ability to fit into any situation. Hank retained the bones of bebop but refined and softened the music. The endless, aggressive rush of notes was still there when needed but enhanced with an awareness of space and melody. The *New York Times* described Hank as "an extraordinary musician" who embodied "the idea of grace under pressure, where assurance and relaxation mask nearly impossible improvisations" (Peter Watrous, 7 December 1989).

Henry Jones was born in Vicksburg, Mississippi, on 31 July 1918 and grew up in Michigan. Two of his brothers became well-known jazzmen, trumpeter Thad and drummer Elvin. Hank began playing piano at an early age and at 13 was working professionally. Initially influenced by stride pianists such as Art Tatum, he became a convert to bebop when working in New York, although elements of stride remained part of his style.

Hank spent much of his early career as a sideman to a roster of illustrious performers such as Benny Goodman, Coleman Hawkins, Wes Montgomery, Charlie Parker and Artie Shaw. Like Tommy Flanagan, he was the "go to guy" when a pianist was wanted for a date. He was also a sought after accompanist, working with Ella Fitzgerald from 1947-53.

From the 1970s, Jones had more opportunities to record under his own name, producing numerous solo, duo and trio discs. Good examples of his trio work are *I Remember You* (1977) and *Compassion* (1978). The reservation I have about many of the trio dates is that Hank can be over-generous with the space he gives to his sidemen.

Teaming up with another pianist of taste and finesse, the Modern Jazz Quartet's John Lewis, Hank made a duo record in 1979 appropriately titled *An Evening with Two Grand Pianos*. Two other elegant duo recordings were with Tommy Flanagan, *Our Delights* (1978) and *I'm All Smiles* (1983).

Hank is at his best on his own and recorded a number of superior solo albums: *Hank* (1976), *Satin Doll* (1976) and *Tiptoe Tapdance* (1978), the title of the last an apt reference to his keyboard style. A highlight of Jones' solo output was his 1992 performance in the famous Concord label Maybeck Hall series. In the notes, Leonard Feather sums it up well: "Hank, like most other pianists of the day, was strongly impressed by Bud Powell, but like Tommy Flanagan and others in the Detroit area, he transcended the bop idiom to become an eclectic interpreter of everything from time-proof ballads to swing and bop standards". His powers showing little sign of fading, Hank recorded two solo discs in Japan in 2004, *'Round Midnight* and *My Funny Valentine*.

Hank Jones died on 16 May 2010 aged 91.

26. LEE KONITZ (1927-2020)

Lee Konitz was born in Chicago on 13 October 1927. His parents were European Jewish emigres. Konitz learnt clarinet and tenor saxophone as a child before finally settling on alto. After briefly working in swing bands, he met blind pianist Lennie Tristano in 1946, the beginning of a significant association. Konitz came under Tristano's influence when bebop was at its height. Tristano had a very different approach. He believed that jazz should be cool and unemotional, with the emphasis on abstract intellectual improvisation. The drummer was to provide an undeviating, metronomic beat. Konitz was instructed to play with a neutral, vibrato-less, pale tone (he wrote a song called "Palo Alto"). If all of this sounds off-putting, it often was, not assisted by Lennie's uncompromising experimentation with concepts like free jazz. Nonetheless, Tristano could swing. This is very much in evidence on a live set from 1955 with Konitz and a tight rhythm section, Gene Ramey and Art Taylor, recorded in that authentically Chinese venue, the Sing Song Room at the Confucius Restaurant in New York. Konitz and Tristano are in superb form throughout.

The Tristano influence is evident on Konitz's first record under his own name, *Subconscious-Lee* (all his life he had terrible weakness for puns, "Sound-Lee", "Deep-Lee", "Pop Goes the Leesel", "Ice Cream Konitz", and so on irritating-lee). All the musicians are Tristano disciples and Lennie lifts the tracks from 1949 he plays on, showing why he inspired such admiration. Although Konitz solos superbly, he is caught in the straight jacket of the Tristano sound: monotonous, chant-like, anaemic.

Konitz worked intermittently with Tristano until the 1960s. He found the inward-looking, cult-like atmosphere of the Tristano school increasingly constricting and decided to break free. Tristano responded by disowning him as a traitor.

Although he acknowledged Charlie Parker as an influence, Konitz was one of the few altoists to create an alternative style. From Tristano came the emphasis on unadorned, linear improvisation. Konitz's technical virtuosity and teeming musical imagination allowed him to create endlessly flowing, logically structured solos. His purity of tone fitted in with Tristano's theories but was his own. Konitz's early playing has a silkiness but also a touch of astringency to add spice. Altoists Paul Desmond and Art Pepper were influenced by him.

Konitz soon built a reputation, playing on Miles Davis' famous *Birth of the Cool* album. He spent some time in the early 1950s as a member of Stan Kenton's orchestra. In January 1953, Konitz sat in with the Gerry Mulligan-Chet Baker Quartet at a club in Los Angeles. Fortunately, the occasion was recorded and, supplemented with some studio tracks, released as *Konitz Meets Mulligan*. The producer of the CD reissue, Michael Cuscuna, comments that, away from Kenton's "confining, pompous, ponderous" band, Konitz "excelled and soared with an inspired fluency and lucidity that had never before been fully realised in his work".

Two enjoyable Konitz albums from 1956 are *Worthwhile* and *Inside Hi-Fi*. The next year he recorded *Tranquillity* in the studio and *The Real Lee Konitz* at a bar in New York – and, yes, it is the real thing, to my mind his finest album. In 1959, Konitz and another Tristano disciple, tenor sax player Warne Marsh, made a live recording at the Half Note club with Bill Evans deputising for Lennie. Marsh sounds dour to the point of sour, but Konitz's playing is smoking hot.

Konitz fell out of favour in the 1960s, being unfairly criticised for being too bloodless. Perhaps as a reaction, his work became more experimental. He immersed himself in the *avant-garde* and his tone became harsher. I prefer the joyous, airy sound of his early music. Many critics rate *Motion*, an uncompromisingly innovative trio record Konitz made with drummer Elvin Jones in 1961, as one of the essential jazz records. While I can appreciate the artistry, I find it difficult to listen to, and, for me, jazz is all about enjoyment. Mozart understood the need for balance, saying of some of his early piano concertos: "There are passages in them from which connoisseurs alone can derive satisfaction, but there are also passages written in such a way that the less learned cannot fail to be pleased". For better or worse, Motion set the direction for Konitz's later output.

Never complacent and with a hunger for innovation and challenge, Konitz played and recorded copiously in every possible situation. He was still performing in his 80s. The *Guardian*'s jazz critic John Fordham observed: "Konitz can sound a little querulous these days, but he approaches every playing situation as if its volatility and seductive potential were still a thrill, and his cliché-avoiding reflexes are as sharp as ever" (7 May 2010). Lee Konitz died on 15 April 2020, as a result of pneumonia brought on by COVID-19.

27. JOHN LEWIS (1920-2001)

John Aaron Lewis was born on 3 May 1920 in Illinois and grew up in New Mexico. Playing piano from the age of seven, he was influenced by the classical masters as well as jazz. Lewis graduated from the University of New Mexico, majoring in music and anthropology, and later took a Master's degree at the Manhattan School of Music.

In 1945, Lewis moved to New York. He was present at the creation of bebop, being hired by "Dizzy" Gillespie as pianist and arranger. As well as working with Diz's big band, Lewis played on many seminal bop sessions with luminaries such as Charlie Parker, Miles Davis and JJ Johnson. He had a different style to other bop pianists such as "Bud" Powell. Lewis' playing was spare and precise with strikingly clear articulation; he had the technique but preferred to avoid the showpieces.

Also in the Gillespie rhythm section were bassist Ray Brown and drummer Kenny Clarke. With Milt Jackson, the first and greatest bop vibraphonist, they would often play as a unit during concerts to give the rest of the band a chance to recover from the stratospheric climaxes it was famous for. Soon they began working on their own. With Percy Heath replacing Brown, they became the Modern Jazz Quartet in 1952. Three years later, "Connie" Kay replaced Clarke and this line up stayed together until 1974. Kay was a versatile musician who could lay down a driving beat or add subtle colouration through a variety of percussion effects. He worked with Paul Desmond in the 1960s and later recorded with Van Morrison, most famously on "Tupelo Honey".

Lewis was the MJQ's musical director, guiding influence and main composer. He and Jackson were, in many ways, musical opposites. Milt's playing was more earthy and blues based. His solos were showers of shimmering notes. Jackson sometimes found Lewis' highly arranged music and fascination with classical forms constricting. However, all four members got along professionally, with individual egos supressed by the collective needs of performance. Their interplay was almost telepathic at times. As Arnold Steinhardt, first violin of the Guarneri String Quartet said of his group, they were "indivisible by four".

The MJQ was very different to the then dominant New York hard bop sound, as its 1955 LPs *Django* and *Concorde* showed. The music was subtle and cerebral, sophisticated and swinging, with an emphasis on ensemble as well as improvisation. Lewis infused jazz performance with "a consciousness of form, using elements of through-composition, counterpoint, melodic variation and, above all, fugue to multiply the trajectories of improvisation" (*Penguin Guide to Jazz*, 8th ed).

A remarkable quality of the MJQ's output is its consistency. There are no really bad records, just some that are less interesting than others. Recommended (in addition to *Django* and *Concorde*) are: *Fontessa* (based on the Italian *commedia dell'arte*), *No Sun in Venice* (from Lewis' soundtrack for the film Sait-on Jamais), *Pyramid*, *Patterns* (the soundtrack from the movie *Odds Against Tomorrow*), *Lonely Woman*, *The Sheriff*, *Collaboration* (with guitarist Laurindo Almeida), *Plays Porgy and Bess*.

A number of live albums show how exciting the MJQ could be in performance. The excellent *European Concert* comes from concerts in Sweden in 1960. Another recording from this tour was released in 1995, dedicated to Connie Kay who died the previous year. This set, in my opinion, has been over-praised, particularly given the poor sound quality. *Blues at Carnegie Hall* is, as the title implies, a swinging, blues-based concert from 1967. Best of all is *The Last Concert*, from November 1974 to mark the group's (temporary as it turned out) break-up. Each member plays at his peak. Many of the MJQ's most famous songs are reprised and in each case the original is surpassed. Whitney Balliett, who wrote about jazz for the *New Yorker* for many years, described the concert as "loose and a little wild. The solos were longer than usual, and they had a singular urgency and brilliance".

The MJQ reformed in 1981 and continued to perform and record intermittently until the 1990s. By now, the group was cruising, albeit very elegantly, occasionally descending into what the *Penguin Guide* aptly describes as "slick Bach-chat". An exception is *For Ellington* from 1988. Inspired by the dedicatee, the Quartet is in top form.

Lewis had a prolific career outside the MJQ. He composed a number of large-scale works attempting to blend jazz and classical music. To me, none of these really come off. I prefer to listen to the former and the latter straight. A review of a 1987 Lewis concert featuring the Quartet and the New York Chamber Symphony described his compositions as "an uneasy straddling of two worlds. The pieces on the program used a small, stodgy palette of classical devices – minor key fugues, four square rhythms, and circle of fifths chord sequences. But with the Quartet, Mr Lewis let loose his sense of harmony and texture" (*New York Times*, 23 June 1987).

Lewis was involved in the 1950s "third stream" movement, an attempt to fuse jazz and classical into a new kind of music. It now seems quaint and over-earnest, a sort of jazz cultural cringe. The results are often as tedious, in their own way, as are the efforts of Ornette Coleman and other exponents of free jazz. Max Harrison, well known as a jazz and classical critic, has perceptively noted that Lewis was "a melodist and orchestrator rather than a designer" whose "writing for large ensembles has rarely matched his arrangements for the MJQ" (M Harrison, A Morgan, R Atkins, M James, J Cooke eds, *Modern Jazz, 1945-70: the essential records*, Aquarius Books, 1975).

More interesting are Lewis' jazz recordings away from the MJQ. *Grand Encounter* from 1956 documents a felicitous meeting between Lewis and Percy Heath and three west coast musicians, guitarist Jim Hall, drummer Chico Hamilton and tenor player Bill Perkins. The last is forgotten now but was a rising star at the time, with a caressing, expressive sound. In 1960, Lewis recorded *The Wonderful World of Jazz* with a quartet, sextet and larger ensemble. The music ranges effortlessly through a cross-section of styles and features some notable soloists, including Ellingtonian Paul Gonsalves.

Lewis made a number of notable recordings featuring his under-rated but considerable pianistic skills. *The John Lewis Piano*, a series of intriguing duo and trio recordings from 1957, is marred by muddy sound. More satisfactory is *Improvised Meditations and Excursions*, a trio record from two years later. In 1979, Lewis toured and recorded as a duo with pianist Hank Jones, a more conventionally boppish player but one who shared Lewis' good taste and restrained elegance.

Lewis made an admirable solo record, *Private Concert*, in 1990. He returned to the format in 1999 with *Evolution*. The *Penguin Guide* commented that it "underscores what an extraordinary figure Lewis was in jazz for over 50 years. Moving yet wonderfully fresh and unaffected, this is a consummate recital by the master". Lewis' last album, *Evolution II*, recorded the following year, is just as good.

Serious, disciplined and focussed, Lewis was never complacent and always critical of his own efforts. He told an interviewer: "You have to communicate as clearly and as correctly as you can. In my case, if I make a mistake the audience may not realise it. But I do. And I'm part of the audience too" (*New York Times*, 31 March 2001).

Personally, Lewis was a reserved, family-centred man. A crusade of his was to counter the image of jazz musicians as unreliable, addled addicts, and to take jazz out of the clubs and into the concert halls. John Lewis died of prostate cancer on 29 March 2001.

28. DAVE McKENNA (1930-2008)

While most jazz pianists in the 1950s sounded like "Bud" Powell and many in the 1960s styled themselves after Bill Evans, a small number still played in the old pre-bebop tradition, beating out the rhythm with a strong left hand. Good examples are Ralph Sutton and Dick Hyman, who made some "finger busting" duo records. The greatest of this school and one of the finest jazz pianists is "Big Dave" McKenna.

Although rooted in tradition, McKenna had a distinctive, multi-faceted musical personality. He could play stride piano that "Fats" Waller would have admired but, rather than pounding mechanically with his left hand, created a unique type of bass accompaniment. Dave could switch effortlessly to a lyrical, emotional style that made many of the Bill Evans imitators sound insensitive. His instantly recognisable touch is crystal clear and gossamer light.

Celebrated critic Whitney Balliett called McKenna "the hardest-swinging jazz pianist of all time". Physically, he was "a man-mountain, whose perfect proportions contain a massive eagle's head, a logger's forearms, and hot-dog fingers" (*New Yorker*, 29 January 1979).

David McKenna was born on 30 May 1930 at Woonsocket, Rhode Island. His father was an amateur drummer and his pianist mother encouraged him to play. He began his life as a jazz musician as a teenager and was soon working with top bands such as those of Charlie Ventura and "Woody" Herman. Dave had a long association with another mainstreamer, cornetist Bobby Hackett.

McKenna spent many years in obscurity. He preferred New England to New York and deliberately confined himself to the role of sideman. There were, fortunately, some solo sessions recorded in 1955 and 1963 and reissued on the Fresh Sound label. Self-deprecatingly, McKenna used to describe himself as a bar room pianist who liked to stay close to the melody. He did, but he also did amazing things with it.

Hank O'Neal was the proprietor of Chiaroscuro Records, virtually a one-person outfit which kept the jazz flame flickering in the 1970s. His day job was as a CIA officer. O'Neal heard McKenna and determined to record him. It was a tough assignment:

> I began nagging Dave about making a solo recording and, judging from what I have heard from others, in those days he didn't take kindly to anyone who nagged him so I am lucky I didn't get more than a firm refusal. I nagged some more but

Dave wasn't budging. This guy knew more tunes and played them better than anyone in town and I'd just heard him playing them. All I could do was shake my head in amazement.

Fortunately, Hank's persistence paid off and McKenna recorded excellent solo albums for him in 1973 and 1977. There was also a stomping quartet date in 1974 featuring saxophonist "Zoot" Sims in peak form. Perhaps the best of the Chiaroscuro recordings is *Alone at the Palace*, made in 1977 with veteran violinist Joe Venuti, who died the following year. According to O'Neal, most of the tracks were recorded with

> a couple of rehearsals and then one or two takes. No overdubs. Joe burned up the fast ones and Dave kicked him along all the way. The ballads were all special; lots of verses and unison passages. The two guys worked so well it seemed as though they were reading one another's mind.

Soon after, Carl Jefferson's Concord label signed McKenna. Shrugging off his former reticence, he made a consistently superior sequence of solo records and finally achieved some long overdue recognition. My favourite is Dave's 1990 recording in Concord's famous Maybeck Recital Hall solo piano series, which eventually numbered 42 CDs. According to Cyra McFadden's liner notes:

> The saloon-cocktail player-whatever got down to work, spinning out a melodic line, supporting it with his signature rumbling bass. In his combination of power and delicacy, he makes you imagine a line-backer who's also a microsurgeon. Midway through, he leaned into the keyboard and began to swing. The audience boogied in their chairs. The rest of that afternoon, in Berkeley parlance, was every bit as much of a bliss bomb.

McKenna also recorded with small ensembles for Concord. A productive association was with tenor saxophonist Scott Hamilton. Born in 1954, Hamilton played in the style of Coleman Hawkins and Ben Webster when most of his contemporaries were trying (often unsuccessfully) to sound like John Coltrane. Far from being derivative, Hamilton found inventive things to say in that idiom. McKenna accompanied him on his 1979 album *Tenorshoes* (bad pun, good record). With drummer Jake Hanna, they made two stimulating trio CDs, *No Bass Hit* and *Major League*. McKenna and Hamilton also recorded with cornetist "Ruby" Braff – another mainstream musician who swam powerfully against the tide. In 1997, Dave cut an album of sparkling duets with bop clarinet maestro Buddy DeFranco, *You Must Believe in Swing*.

Big Dave's last record, *An Intimate Evening with Dave McKenna*, was released in 2002. His friend and the album's producer, Gunnar Jacobsen, noted that

> the audience was filled with musicians, something which usually happens at his appearances. They always come to hear his wonderful way of phrasing; how he often re-writes the song without losing the melody; his many medleys (he knows more than any other living pianist); his marvellous left hand, always unpredictable, ranging from single notes through full chords and stride to everything in between. From the first time I heard Dave I was in awe of his playing. This evening was no different, a glorious and intimate evening!

Dave McKenna died of lung cancer on 18 October 2008.

29. JACKIE McLEAN (1931-2006)

Charlie Parker, like Louis Armstrong, had a legion of followers. Many were imitators; a few were innovators in the master's tradition. Of all the post-Parker alto saxophonists, the best was Jackie McLean. Few things in jazz are more stimulating than the whooping, soaring, coruscating Jackie Mac attack.

John Lenwood McLean was born in New York on 17 May 1931. His father was a jazz guitarist and his stepfather owned a record shop where Jackie worked and soaked up jazz. In his youth, his friends and neighbours were jazz aristocracy: "Bud" Powell, "Sonny" Rollins, and Kenny Drew. Charlie Parker was a mentor. Miles Davis hired McLean when he was 20. Like Davis, Jackie was a heroin addict. Miles said of a 1955 date: "Jackie got so high he was terrified he couldn't play. I don't know what all that shit was about but after that I never used Jackie again". In spite of the inauspicious circumstances, *Miles Davis and Milt Jackson Quintet/Sextet* showcases all three soloists in superior form. McLean recorded a number of dates as a leader for the Prestige label in 1956-57, frequently with pianist Mal Waldron. Sometimes denigrated as juvenilia, these are, in fact, superior performances: *Lights Out* and *4, 5 and 6* are good examples.

As well as Davis, other bebop giants were quick to hire McLean. He featured on Charlie Mingus' landmark 1956 LP *Pithecanthropus Erectus*. Mingus composed a ballad feature for him, *Portrait of Jackie*. Under Mingus' influence McLean began to find his own musical voice and his tone acquired its distinctive acid-etched edge. They parted company after a violent argument. According to Derek Ansell's biography of McLean, at a performance in Ohio, Mingus

> began berating Jackie on the stand and kept haranguing him repeatedly, all through the gig. Now most band leaders, if they had a problem with a sideman, would take him aside after the show and take issue with whatever he was doing wrong, in private. Not Mingus. He would blow up in front of an audience. It was all too much for McLean who came off stage and told Mingus he was giving two weeks' notice. This lead to a dreadful altercation where Mingus punched him in the mouth knocking back his two front teeth. The altoist, in a rage by now, attacked Mingus with a knife but somebody hit him on the arm and the bass player received only a minor cut (*Sugar Free Saxophone: the life and music of Jackie McLean*, Northway Publications, 2013).

McLean moved to the physically, if not musically, safer environment of Art Blakey's Jazz Messengers. Jackie and Art were musically and personally compatible, although Blakey relentlessly pushed his young star to perfect his music. McLean's contribution to the Messenger's classic 1956 *Hard Bop* album showed "how effectively he had built upon the darker side of Charlie Parker's world, creating a harsh relentless mode of expression, comprising strident delivery, a strained, occasionally coarse tone" (Michael James in M Harrison, A Morgan, R Atkins, M James, J Cooke eds, *Modern Jazz, 1945-70: the essential records*, Aquarius Books, 1975).

Jackie then signed with the Blue Note label. The quality of his recordings in this period is inconsistent but there is one undisputed masterpiece, *Bluesnik* from 1961. The blues had always been a key element of McLean's music and *Bluesnik* demonstrated his "absorption in fresh means of melodic expression based on freer use of rhythm and harmony; it revealed his tonal power and the emotional edge to his music to be as keen as ever; and it proved that the blues, in their many guises, could hold the listener spellbound" (Michael James in M Harrison, A Morgan, R Atkins, M James, J Cooke eds, *Modern Jazz, 1945-70: the essential records*, Aquarius Books, 1975).

In 1959, McLean performed in Jack Gelber's controversial play *The Connection*, about a group of heroin addicts waiting anxiously for their supplier. The script called for interludes of improvised jazz, and pianist Freddie Redd led a quartet featuring Jackie that performed on stage. The music Redd composed for the play was released on Blue Note and captures McLean at his best.

Jackie found conventional bop harmonies increasingly stifling, to the point where he sometimes hit a brick wall in his solos. This is evident on *Capuchin Swing* from 1960 – the title and a picture on the album cover of *Jackie with a monkey* are a daring, for the times, allusion to his heroin habit. After stunning performances on "Francisco" and "Condition Blue", he sounds uninspired on the rest of the LP. McLean's solution was to follow Ornette Coleman into free jazz, beginning with *Let Freedom Ring* in 1962. There is some great playing but also squawks and squeals I find disconcerting.

In the 1970s, free of his addiction, McLean became heavily involved with music education. He continued to tour and record, often for the Danish Steeplechase label. His son Rene, also a saxophonist, often worked with him. Jackie's later music retreated from the "new thing". As he told an interviewer: "I've grown out of being just a bebop saxophone player, or being a free saxophone player. I don't know where I am now. I guess I'm somewhere mixed up between all the saxophonists who ever played" (*New York Times*, 3 April 2006). Jackie McLean died on 31 March 2006.

30. CHARLES MINGUS (1922-79)

Charles Mingus was born in Texas on 22 April 1922. His father was in the US Army and he grew up in Los Angeles. Originally attracted to the cello, Mingus studied double bass and composition as a teenager. He was prodigiously talented, working with Louis Armstrong, Lionel Hampton, Charlie Parker and Art Tatum in his early career. Mingus was also a skilled pianist, releasing an excellent solo album in 1963, *Mingus Plays Piano: spontaneous compositions and improvisations*. Above all, he was a composer of stature and one of the great jazz innovators.

Gospel and "Duke" Ellington were Mingus' main musical influences: "All the music I heard when I was a child was church music. The blues was in the churches – moaning and riffs between the audience and the preacher. When I first heard Duke Ellington in person, I almost jumped out of the balcony. One piece excited me so much I screamed".

Mingus call his early ensembles "jazz workshops" to emphasise the creative cross-fertilisation of ideas between musicians he sought to achieve. His conception, he said, involved

> nothing being written. I 'write' compositions but only on mental score paper – then I lay out the composition part by part to the musicians. I play them the framework on piano so that they are all familiar with my interpretation and feeling and with the scale and chord progressions to be used. Each man's individual style is taken into consideration, both in ensemble and solos. In this way I find it possible to keep my own compositional flavour in the pieces and yet to allow the musicians more individual freedom.

Mingus was a forceful musical and physical presence in any group he played with. He had a propulsive, booming sound that drove his musicians relentlessly. Just under six foot and solidly built, Mingus had a violent temper. His career is littered with accounts of physical attacks on fellow musicians, unruly audience members, and just about anyone else who annoyed him. Long-time trombonist in Mingus' band, Jimmy Knepper, had a tooth punched out by him when a musical disagreement turned physical. Derek Ansell has described Mingus as

> at one minute a towering, aggressive monster and a threat to anybody obstructing his path and the next a quiet, sensitive musician, fashioning a tender ballad on his bass or driving an excruciatingly intense up-tempo jazz composition … Always inventive and original, Mingus' music was fresh, challenging, incomprehensible to some, the latest and greatest

to others (*Sugar Free Saxophone: the life and music of Jackie McLean*, Northway Publications, 2013).

Pithecanthropus Erectus from 1956 was Mingus' first masterpiece – astonishing for the time and still momentous music. He chose excellent soloists in Jackie McLean, the unjustly neglected JR Monterose on tenor, and pianist Mal Waldron. The theme of the lengthy title piece is ambitious: the story of humanity from the first person to walk erect to the extinction of the race due to vanity and greed. Conventional ensemble passages alternate with free improvisation. McLean's banshee wails are a particularly effective accompaniment to the destruction of *homo sapiens*.

The second half of the 1950s saw Mingus at his peak, with one classic following another. *Tijuana Moods*, recorded in 1957 but not released until 1962, is a vivid tone poem chronicling a trip to Mexico. According to Mingus, who called it his best record, the music was written

> during a very blue period in my life. I was minus a wife and in flight to forget her with an expected dream in Tijuana. I decided to benefit musically from this experience and set out to compose and re-create what I saw around me. It included a strip tease in one of the many local night clubs. 'Ysabel's Table Dance' sums up all you could buy in Tijuana.

Another memorable track is "Los Mariachis", with its infectious Latin melody. It portrays a group of street musicians who followed Mingus, playing "everything from barrel house to a stiff attempt at the blues" to get a tip. *Tijuana Moods* marked the debut of two of Mingus' longest-serving collaborators, trombonist Jimmy Knepper and drummer Dannie Richmond.

East Coasting, recorded soon after Tijuana Moods with a similar personnel, featured Bill Evans on piano. Although not as well-known, it is another considerable achievement, with a cool, moody ambience.

In 1959, Mingus made his most famous record, *Mingus Ah Um*. It included his two best-known compositions, the gospel influenced "Better Get it in Your Soul" and a lament for Lester Young, "Goodbye Pork Pie Hat". The music has been described as kaleidoscopic:

> The horns evolve ever-changing textures, ensembles alternating with solos to produce a continuous impression of mobility and inventiveness. It is worth remarking how wide a range of melodic material is employed in these compositions. Certainly there are not many LPs that comprise traditional elements, swing riffs, gospel lines and sequences anticipating the work of such as Albert Ayler. All these are mysteriously welded into a whole (Michael James in M Harrison, A Morgan, R Atkins, M James, J Cooke eds, *Modern Jazz, 1945-70: the essential records*, Aquarius Books, 1975).

Mingus Dynasty (he had Chinese ancestry), also recorded in 1959, has been overshadowed by its predecessor but bubbles over with creativity.

In the 1960s, Mingus was influenced by the free jazz movement, hiring the cacophonous saxophonist Eric Dolphy. Almost every critic lists *The Black Saint and the Sinner Lady*, a large scale suite from 1963, as Mingus' finest work. While I can appreciate the strengths – orchestral passages worthy of Ellington, melodic interludes, brilliant solos from altoist Charlie Mariano – I've always been ambivalent about the discordant free jazz sections. More accessible is *Mingus, Mingus, Mingus, Mingus, Mingus*, recorded about the same time with a similar ensemble, which robustly reprises some of his most famous compositions.

Mingus flirted with rock, recording *Three or Four Shades of Blues* in 1977 with electric guitarists Larry Coryell and Philip Catherine. It is a sad travesty, revealing a failing compositional talent in the lengthy title piece. Mingus was increasingly affected by motor neurone disease which claimed him on 5 January 1979.

31. THELONIOUS MONK (1917-1982)

Thelonious Monk was a great pianist and a great eccentric. Quirky, insular and withdrawn, he occasionally got up from the keyboard and danced on stage like a shuffling bear. Monk played in his own uncompromisingly unconventional way and waited for the world to catch up with him – it took a while. He was also a significant composer, with standards like "Round Midnight" and "Blue Monk" to his credit.

Thelonious Sphere Monk was born in North Carolina on 10 October 1917. He brought to jazz "a musical sensibility from the black church, a study of sacred music (later recording the hymn 'Abide with Me'), a love of Rachmaninoff and Chopin, and a mastery of the by then archaic, two-handed stride piano style". Monk's playing "with its crunchy dissonances, forceful attack, open spaces, and off-kilter rhythms, has deeply imprinted itself on other instrumentalists and vocalists" (David A Graham, *The Atlantic*, 18 October 2017).

Monk began playing jazz in his teenage years and became the house pianist at Minton's, a Manhattan club frequented by the pioneers of bebop, although he was never a conventional bopper. Alfred Lion of Blue Note Records and his wife Lorraine recognised Monk's talent and recorded him from 1947-52 even though the sales were minimal. They are uneven records, with sometimes very uneven accompanists, but Monk's solos shine through.

In the early 1950s Monk recorded for the Prestige label with growing critical recognition but continuing public indifference. The best of the series is a CD combining trio sessions from 1952 and 1954. Unfortunately, the appallingly recorded piano sounds like a harpsichord – an instrument conductor Sir Thomas Beecham memorably described as like "two skeletons copulating on a tin roof in a thunderstorm".

In 1955, Monk found a sympathetic home when he signed with Orrin Keepnews' Riverside Records. It inaugurated his most creative period. To combat the perception that Monk's music was "difficult", Keepnews had him record an LP of standards and one of Ellington compositions. The latter is a classic.

Monk's first masterpiece, with a few rough edges, is *Brilliant Corners* released in 1957. Four of the five numbers are Monk originals played by a quintet including "Sonny" Rollins on tenor saxophone. The title track is one of Monk's most complex compositions. Keepnews recalled that the musicians struggled and concentrated and shook their heads over some passages with those half smiles that mean: 'Hard? This is impossible!' They worked hard also because Monk's creativity never stands still: during a preliminary run through of a number, between takes or even during one, changes of phrasing or of detail will evolve, as a constant fusion of arrangement and improvisation keeps taking place. And Monk is a hard taskmaster at a recording session, a perfectionist. In the end it wasn't impossible – merely far from easy, and everyone else was satisfied and Monk probably almost satisfied.

Monk's Music from 1958 is even better. The front line featured young and old lions of the tenor saxophone, John Coltrane and Coleman Hawkins. Again, it was a difficult record to make: Monk collapsed at the end of the first day's recording with nothing usable on tape. Fortunately, everything clicked into place the next day. As well as long versions of Monk's "Well, You Needn't" and "Epistrophy" by the septet, Hawkins plays superbly on "Ruby, My Dear" with the rhythm section only. "Crepuscule with Nellie" (dedicated to Monk's wife) has an appropriate twilight glow. Monk plays a pellucid solo followed by Coltrane at his most emotive.

In 1957, Monk formed a short-lived quartet with Coltrane. Its music was poorly documented until a good quality live recording from a Carnegie Hall concert was discovered in the Library of Congress and issued in 2005. Both are in excellent form, their very individual styles complementing each other. Monk's spare utterances are like stepping-stones in the fast flowing stream of Coltrane's playing.

Monk excelled at that most difficult art, solo piano. Keepnews recorded him twice in this format, *Thelonious Himself* (1957) and

Alone in San Francisco (1959). Both have a predominantly lyrical feel as Monk slowly and reflectively picks his way through a collection of standards.

By the end of the 1950s, "the times were beginning to catch up with Monk, for a generation well-versed in the search for fresh harmonic relationships through their experience of hard bop, and stimulated by that style's rhythmic devices, found themselves with a key to his music". As the new decade began, Monk was "almost at rest after a long uphill haul, and just before the long slide down" (Jack Cooke in M Harrison, A Morgan, R Atkins, M James, J Cooke, *Modern Jazz, 1945-70: the essential records*, Aquarius Books, 1975). In 1962, Monk signed with Columbia – big label, big publicity, relatively big money. Two years later, he made the cover of *Time* magazine. Monk's records sold well but became increasingly predictable. A highlight is a collection of his solo piano pieces, *Monk Alone: the Complete Solo Studio Recordings 1962–1968*.

Increasingly beset by mental and physical health problems, Monk became reclusive in the 1970s, retreating from recording and performing. He died of a stroke on 17 February 1982.

32. WES MONTGOMERY (1923-1968)

Probably the best known jazz guitarist after Charlie Christian is Wes Montgomery. He was an exceptional improviser with a warm, opulent sound that was uniquely his own. This was partly due to the fact that he plucked the strings with his thumb rather than using a plectrum. A typical Montgomery solo consisted of fluent single notes, octave runs, then block chords that generated an exciting climax. He often turned the amplification down, highlighting his pristine single string work. Wes' playing combined

the rhythmic assurance of Charlie Christian, the romantic passion of Django Reinhardt and the unruffled poise of Jimmy Raney. He is the one post-war guitarist fully capable of exploiting the range of his instrument by delineating the different registers: it is characteristic of him to play long passages in the deep, mellow bottom register and then to sweep up-wards to his ringing top notes with a beautiful sense of timing (Ronald Atkins in M Harrison, A Morgan, R Atkins, M James, J Cooke, *Modern Jazz, 1945-70: the essential records*, Aquarius Books, 1975).

John Leslie "Wes" Montgomery was born in Indianapolis on 6 March 1923. He taught himself to play guitar in his late teens. Wes came from a musical family and his brothers "Buddy" (piano and vibes) and Monk (bass) were both accomplished jazz musicians. *Far Wes* from 1958 features all three brothers in excellent form.

Wes worked briefly with Lionel Hampton's band but spent most of the 1950s, when he was in his musical prime, in his hometown. He disliked touring and had a family of eight to support. Wes had a day job as a welder and played in local clubs at night. It was in one of these that "Cannonball" Adderley heard him and was so impressed that he persuaded Orrin Keepnews to sign him for his Riverside label.

In 1960, Montgomery made arguably his best record, *Incredible Jazz Guitar*, with Tommy Flanagan on piano, bassist Percy Heath and drummer Albert Heath. *So Much Guitar* from the following year isn't far behind. In December 1961 Montgomery recorded with the Modern Jazz Quartet's vibraphonist Milt Jackson. Keepnews re-called that, although they had never worked together before, there was an

> uncanny rapport between the two leaders. Of course, they had many attitudes and attributes in common. If the blues is in-deed a language, it is one in which these men were extremely fluent. Equally important to both was the melodic content of their music. There is an extraordinary richness and fullness to their performances here, and there is also a feeling that each

man is somehow drawing something tangible from the other's performance.

In 1962, Keepnews decided to record Montgomery live. He thought that Wes, who tended to be nervous and insecure, might be more relaxed outside the studio. On 25 June, Wes and an outstanding band assembled at a coffee house in Berkeley: Johnny Griffin on tenor sax, pianist Wynton Kelly, bassist Paul Chambers, and "Philly" Joe Jones on drums. At the time, the rhythm section was with Miles Davis and later worked as the Wyn Kelly Trio. The night's performance, released as *Full House*, did not disappoint. Griffin scorches, Kelly swings, and Wes scintillates throughout.

In the mid-1960s, Montgomery signed with the Verve label and made a "lucrative but aesthetically sterile series of LPs on which he strums resignedly while violins twitter around him" (Ronald Atkins in M Harrison, A Morgan, R Atkins, M James, J Cooke, *Modern Jazz, 1945-70: the essential records*, Aquarius Books, 1975). One exception to this mushy musical miasma is *Smokin' at the Half Note*, recorded in 1965 with the Wyn Kelly Trio. Only two tracks on the original album were from the Half Note performances. Producer Creed Taylor was unhappy with the standard of the rest and got the band into the studio to cut three more titles. The quality of the LP is uniformly high, with Wes and Wyn sparking each other to ever greater achievement. A live recording has recently emerged of Wes guesting with the Kelly trio in 1966, *Smokin' in Seattle*. Montgomery again plays with vigour and invention – although it is as much a showcase for the underrated Kelly, who died in 1971 at the age of 39.

Wes Montgomery was a retiring family man who did not abuse alcohol or drugs, although he was a heavy smoker. He died of a massive heart attack at home in Indianapolis on 15 June 1968.

33. GERRY MULLIGAN (1927-1996)

West coast jazz emerged as a genre in the 1950s as an alternative to New York hard bop. It was cool, laid-back and mainly white. There was an emphasis on arrangements and attempts to integrate classical elements into jazz – mediocre concertos and suites abounded. To me, the west coast sound is often anaemic and over-elaborate. However, it did produce some influential soloists: Stan Getz, Jimmy Giuffre, Art Pepper, "Bud" Shank, and Gerry Mulligan. The last was the archetypal west coast musician.

Gerald Joseph Mulligan was born in New York on 6 April 1927. He had a peripatetic childhood as his father was an engineer whose work took him all over the US. Gerry began working as a saxophonist in his teens but had more early success as an arranger, writing for Gene Krupa, Claude Thornhill and Stan Kenton. In his arrangements he "studiously avoided the clichés of big band orchestration, opting instead for a well-centred, calmly rational approach. And he made sure that many of his arrangements were full of moving lines, not only referring to an earlier style of polyphonic jazz, but also making his arrangements sound almost improvised" (*New York Times*, 21 January 1996). Mulligan was one of the few virtuoso baritone saxophonists in jazz; he had a light tone that could sometimes be mistaken for tenor. Gerry was also a competent – but no more than that – pianist.

While with Claude Thornhill, Gerry became friendly with arranger Gil Evans. With Miles Davis they recorded *The Birth of the Cool* in 1949-50 with a group of like-minded musicians including Lee Konitz and John Lewis. The aim was to restore the role of the ensemble which boppers like Charlie Parker almost completely ignored in their head-long rush into incandescent solos. *The Birth of the Cool* was not a commercial success at the time but its stature has grown immensely and it now defines the west coast sound. Participation in these sessions helped establish Mulligan's reputation as a soloist and arranger.

In 1952, Gerry moved to Los Angeles and teamed up with trumpeter "Chet" Baker, an instantly compatible combination. The gruff chuffing of Mulligan's baritone provided the perfect foil for Baker's pure sound. Mulligan did not to use a pianist, a radical step at the time. Their music had a "freshness of conception which the years have not dimmed. Mulligan chose his men with care, and in Baker was lucky to find a young, completely natural trumpeter with a lovely tone. The quartet is a masterly example of internal balance" (Alun Morgan in M Harrison, A Morgan, R Atkins, M James, J Cooke, *Modern Jazz, 1945-70: the essential records*, Aquarius Books, 1975).

Both Mulligan and Baker were heroin addicts. In 1953, the police raided the house they were living in and arrested them and their wives. Mulligan took the rap and did time – it was the end of the quartet. They did, however, make a reunion record in 1957 that recaptured much of the old interplay.

Baker formed a quartet with the elegant pianist Russ Freeman which recorded a classic LP in 1953. He was also popular as a singer, with a limited but intimate style. Baker's addiction led him into a downward spiral culminating in his still mysterious end. In 1988, he was found dead on the pavement below his hotel room in Amsterdam.

Mulligan kicked his habit. In 1954 he recorded *California Concerts*, two sparkling sets reissued in full on CD in 1988. The first featured a quartet with the accomplished but otherwise unknown Jon Eardley on trumpet. The other introduced a multi-talented sextet, also featuring Eardley plus "Zoot" Sims on tenor sax and Bob Brookmeyer on valve trombone. Brookmeyer was a proficient pianist – he recorded a duo album with Bill Evans in 1959 without being disgraced. A 1955 LP by the sextet integrated Mulligan's arranging and performing skills to great effect.

In 1956, Gerry returned to the piano-less quartet format, with Brookmeyer instead of Baker. Having two such brown-sounding instruments in the front line should have been monotonous. Instead, a live set at Boston's Storyville club showed a "romping self-confidence. For all the buttoned-down sobriety of this group. It is also a fleet and powerful outfit, capable of generating a big resonant sound" (*Penguin Guide to Jazz*, 8th ed).

Mulligan signed with Norman Granz's Verve label in the late 1950s. Granz loved to combine big names and Mulligan made a series of LPs where he "met" just about anyone that Norman could lay hands on, including Ellingtonians Johnny Hodges and Ben Webster, and Dave Brubeck's altoist, Paul Desmond. Gerry provided a good assessment of the quality of these sessions: "I dug the date with Johnny Hodges and, of course, the original one with Paul Desmond. I didn't nearly enjoy the one with Stan Getz as much. That was more forced and more exclusively the idea of Norman Granz. He wanted that date, he wanted it a lot more than I did. It would be fair to say that I place the one with Ben Webster as the best of the lot". In 1962, Mulligan and Desmond reunited to record the excellent *Two of a Mind* for RCA.

An unlikely meeting was between Mulligan and Thelonious Monk in 1957. When Riverside Records owner and producer Orrin Keepnews learnt that the two were friends he got them into the studio. It proved to be a very productive session despite the disparate backgrounds: east coast eccentric meets cool, crew-cut Californian.

In the 1960s Mulligan led a large ensemble, the Concert Jazz Band. The studio arrangements were sometimes over-complex but the band really swung in performance, as *Live at the Village Vanguard* from December 1960 shows. The ensemble passages pack a punch and Mulligan solos with passion.

From the late 1960s until the early '70s, Mulligan often worked with Dave Brubeck, proving to be a compatible replacement for Paul Desmond. *Live at the Berlin Philharmonie* (1970) is a good example of this outfit in action. Mulligan out-swings Brubeck with his bluesy earthiness.

Mulligan remained active until the end of his life although the pace slowed, the quality diminished, and there was a tendency to re-live old glories – we've all got it in us, I know. Already battling liver cancer, Gerry Mulligan died on 20 January 1968 of complications after knee surgery.

34. "RED" NICHOLS (1905-1965)

Although it is not fashionable to mention it in this age of inverse racism, there was an influential school of white jazz in the 1920s. Jean Goldkette and Ben Pollack led popular, swinging bands that contained fine musicians. On 13 October 1926, at the Roseland Ballroom in Manhattan, the Goldkette organisation went up against Fletcher Henderson's orchestra, the toast of Harlem, in a battle of the bands. Henderson trumpeter Rex Stewart, later an Ellington stalwart, admitted "those little tight-ass white boys creamed us" (Ken Burns and Geoffrey Ward, *Jazz: a history of America's music*, Pimlico, 2001).

Many of the stars of the Goldkette and Pollack bands and other up-and-coming performers gathered in New York in the 1920s, then, as now, the proving (killing?) ground for young musicians on the make. The New York school created some memorable jazz. Its best-known exponent is cornetist and trumpeter "Red" Nichols.

Ernest Loring Nichols was born in Utah on 8 May 1905. His father taught music and led a brass band, which featured Red at age 12. Soon after he was playing jazz. Arriving in New York in 1923, Red's industry, reliability and ability quickly established him as a major figure. He is estimated to have played on something like 4,000 recordings in the 1920s. Nichols was very much in the "Bix" Beiderbecke tradition. He was a superb technician but did not indulge in lengthy, bravura breaks, preferring to dart in and out of the ensemble. His solos were clipped, elegant phrases that glowed like small jewels.

Red's best-known band was the Five Pennies (five pennies in a nickel, get it?). It featured a galaxy of talent, notably "Miff" Mole, a pioneer of the jazz trombone. One of Miff's disciples, Glenn Miller, was a soloist and arranger. Jimmy Dorsey contributed excellent alto sax and clarinet. Adrian Rollini played the unwieldy bass saxophone and made it sound graceful. "Pee Wee" Russell was an original, eccentric clarinettist. Other regulars were violinist Joe Venuti and guitarist Eddie Lang, jazz trailblazers on their respective instruments.

Nichols' music was nimble and buoyant, with a subtle swing, although the rhythm could sound stiff at times. Jazz scholar Dan Morgenstern has noted that it featured "highly sophisticated ensemble playing, intricate harmonic schemes, and brilliant instrumental displays". Nichols was immensely popular in Europe and America. "Ida, Sweet as Apple Cider" was a number one US hit in 1927, selling over a million copies.

A talented group of musicians came to New York in the late 1920s from Chicago. "Bud" Freeman was an innovative tenor saxophonist with a light, serpentine style. Elements of Bud's music can be heard in Stan Getz and Scott Hamilton. Also from Chicago was

Gene Krupa, who played a crucial role in the evolution of the jazz drummer from time-keeper to soloist. His family wanted him to study for the priesthood but he decided on jazz. Given Krupa's wild man personality, he made the right choice. Another of the Chicagoans was a young clarinettist named Benny Goodman. They brought a hotter, harder approach to New York jazz. Recognising their talent, Nichols hired them.

Red also hired Texan Jack Teagarden, the "king of the blues trombone", who arrived in New York in 1927. Like others trying to make it, he had a depressingly tough time. "Big T" sang with feeling in "Makin' Friends": "I'd rather drink muddy water, Lord, sleep in a hollow log, than to be up here in New York, treated like a dirty dog".

The new boys super-charged Nichols' music. A session in July 1930 with Goodman, Teagarden and Krupa produced some exhilarating sides: "Sweet Georgia Brown", "China Boy", and "Shim-Me-Sha-Wabble". With those three plus Freeman, Nichols recorded two more classic tracks the next month: "Carolina in the Morning" (with a memorable Glenn Miller arrangement) and "Who". Red finished the year with an all-star session in December, featuring trumpeter "Wingy" Manone (he had one arm), Miller, Goodman and Krupa. "How Come You Do Me Like You Do?" and "Corrine Corrina" are masterpieces, with catchy vocals from Harold Arlen and Wingy respectively.

Red led a big band in the later 1930s, then joined the Army in World War Two. He re-formed the Five Pennies after the war. The arrangements tended to be bland but his graceful, melodious solos shine through. In 1959, he was portrayed by Danny Kaye in a movie loosely based on his life, The Five Pennies. It revived Nichols' career. He was playing a lucrative gig at one of the big hotels in Las Vegas when he died of a heart attack on 28 June 1965.

35. CHARLIE PARKER (1920-55)

In the 1940s, a radically different type of jazz emerged called bebop. The name is said to be a verbal rendering of a typical phrase in the new style. Reacting against the orthodoxies of the big bands, bop was furious and frantic, with vestigial arrangements. After a few perfunctory ensemble choruses, the soloists took over with angular flurries of notes. Most Swing and New Orleans musicians hated it, but for the young and hip it was a messianic revelation.

The greatest of the boppers, and one of the most transcendent of jazz soloists, was Charlie "Bird" Parker. Poet and jazz critic Philip Larkin has commented that Parker "found jazz chugging along in 4/4 time in the tonic and dominant, and splintered it into a thousand rhythmic and harmonic pieces. Showers of sixteenths, accented on half and quarter beats, exhibited a new harmonic fecundity and an originality of phrasing that had scarcely been hinted at before" (*All What Jazz*, Faber, 1985).

Born on 29 August 1920, **Charles Parker** grew up in Kansas City, Missouri. His father was a vaudeville performer who also worked as a Pullman chef and waiter. He disappeared from Charlie's life at an early age. The young Parker found direction and fulfilment in music. His indulgent mother bought him an alto saxophone when he was 11 and he was soon practising up to 15 hours a day. Parker left high school to become a professional musician in 1935.

Kansas City was well-known for its gangs, corruption, night life and jazz. Bird frequented the jazz clubs (as did future President Harry Truman) and was particularly influenced by "Count" Basie and his star tenor saxophonist, Lester Young. Parker's first significant job was with KC stride pianist Jay "Hootie" McShann's band.

In New York in the mid-1940s Parker was hanging out and jamming with the pioneers of bebop, trumpeter "Dizzy" Gillespie, pianist "Bud" Powell and drummer Max Roach. In 1945, he began recording with his own small group. Parker quickly became a sensation, astounding everyone who heard him. For many fans and musicians, jazz was never the same again. Pianist Hampton Hawes recalled:

> I couldn't believe what he was doing, how anyone could so totally block out everything extraneous, light a fire that hot inside him and constantly feed on that fire. Those of us who were affected the strongest felt we'd be willing to do anything

to warm ourselves by that fire, get some of that grease pumping in our veins. He f….d up all our minds. It was where the ultimate truth was (Hampton Hawes with Don Asher, *Raise up off Me: a portrait of Hampton Hawes*, Coward, McCann and Geoghegan, 1974).

The doyen of jazz critics, Whitney Balliett, said in a perceptive profile in the *New Yorker* that Parker could do "anything he liked with time, and in his ballads he lagged behind the beat, floated easily along on it, or leapt ahead of it". The blues lived "in every room of his style, and he was one of the most striking and affecting blues improvisers we have had". He used "multitudes of notes but never a superfluous one. His runs exploded like light spilling out an opened door. His rhythms had a muscled, chattering density". Parker's tone could be "edgy and even sharp. It could be smooth and big and sombre. It could be soft and husky" (1 March 1976).

Almost as spectacular as Parker's playing was his private life:

> He was a baffling and extraordinary drug addict – one who, unlike most addicts, was also a glutton, an alcoholic, and a man of insatiable sexual needs. He would eat 20 hamburgers in a row, drink 16 double whiskies in a couple of hours, and go to bed with two women at once. At times, he went berserk, and would throw his saxophone out a hotel window or walk into the ocean in a brand-new suit.

An "irresistibly attractive man", Parker "bit almost every hand that fed him" (Whitney Balliett, *New Yorker*, 1 March 1976).

Parker's discography, like his lifestyle, is chaotic. Record companies have ferreted out and released every last note he recorded. Often, it adds little (except to the price) and should have stayed in the vault. There are three main bodies of studio work. In November

1945 Parker began recording for the Savoy label. The quality is uneven and some of the sides with Swing-era musicians such as "Tiny" Grimes and "Slim" Gaillard are grotesque. The first Savoy session in November 1945 could hardly be described as polished but produced classics such as "KoKo" and "Now's the Time". Parker astutely hired the young Miles Davis. Although still mastering his instrument, Miles provided a smooth, fluent contrast to Bird's volcanic playing. The 1947-48 sessions, also with Davis, are more consistent and resulted in some of Parker best solos: "Chasin' the Bird", "Cheryl", "Bluebird", "Constellation", "Parker's Mood".

In 1946-47, Bird made a series of classic recordings for Ross Russell's west coast label, Dial. These sessions had an abrupt, fortunately temporary, interruption when, after a session in July 1946, Parker had a complete breakdown, running naked through the lobby of his hotel and setting fire to his bed. He was committed to a mental institution in California, Camarillo State Hospital, for six months. The last track he cut before his breakdown, "Lover Man", has a haunting intensity. A rejuvenated Parker returned to the studio in 1947 and recorded some of his most serene music: "Relaxin' at Camarillo", "My Old Flame", "Bird of Paradise", "Embraceable You".

Parker next signed with Norman Granz's Verve records. Granz put him in some truly awful settings: a vocal choir, a Latin band, and, of course, with strings. Fortunately, there were also some small groups, including with Dizzy Gillespie. The cream of these is gathered together on the appropriately titled *Bird's Best Bop on Verve*.

The live material is even more disordered, with a large number of poor quality recordings labelled "historic", "legendary", "immortal" etc. One of the best was only rediscovered and issued in 2005, a Parker/Gillespie quintet concert recorded at the Town Hall in New York City in June 1945. Dizzy is in his prime and his playing has all the elements that he was famous for: power, exhilaration, incredible high notes, bravura passages. Able to stretch out more than on a three-minute 78 recording, Parker's solos are electrifying, even for him. A concert at Carnegie Hall in 1947 also has some superlative playing from Bird and Diz but the sound balance is poor, with the drums over-loud and John Lewis' piano virtually inaudible.

From December 1948 to March 1949, Bird had a regular gig at the Royal Roost, a New York club known as the "Metropolitan Bopera House". Some of the weekly radio broadcasts of his performances were recorded and released on Savoy. The sound quality is remarkably good given the circumstances. Parker was with some of his favourite accompanists: Miles Davis then Kenny Dorham on trumpet, pianist Al Haig, Tommy Potter on bass, and drummer Max Roach. In a familiar environment with congenial colleagues and a receptive audience, he is in sublime form on most tracks.

A final flare of Parker's brilliance was a concert in Toronto in May 1953, *Jazz at Massey Hall*, later released as *The Greatest Jazz Concert Ever* – and for once the publicists could claim truth as a defence. As well as Bird, it featured Gillespie, Powell, Roach and Charlie Mingus. Parker played a plastic alto as his regular horn was in the pawn shop. This was the first Parker LP I bought and remains a favourite. On "Perdido" he plays one of the most perfectly constructed solos I have ever heard.

After his stay at Camarillo, Parker quickly reverted to all his old bad habits and by the early 1950s was starting to burn out:

He collapsed on the street, he got into horrendous fights, he tried to commit suicide. He slept, when he slept at all, on floors or in bathtubs or in the beds of friends. He cadged drinks and he panhandled. His horn was usually in hock, and he missed gigs. And at last his playing faltered (Whitney Balliett, *New Yorker*, 1 March 1976).

Charlie Parker died on 12 March 1955 at the age of 34 of the combined effects of cirrhosis, pneumonia, an ulcer, and a heart attack. The surgeon who performed the autopsy estimated his age at between 50 and 60.

36. OSCAR PETERSON (1925-2007)

Oscar Peterson has been the subject of much critical controversy. Some admire his prodigious technique and ability to adapt to any musical situation. Others disparage him as a superficial exhibitionist. I've swayed both ways over the years but have finally come down heavily on the side of the admirers.

Oscar Emanuel Peterson was born in Montreal on 15 August 1925 of West Indian parents. His father was a porter on the Canadian Pacific Railway and an enthusiastic amateur musician who encouraged his son to learn piano. Oscar's sister Daisy, a piano teacher, also nurtured his talent. He later studied with classical pianist, Paul De Marky. Dedicated to his music from an early age, Peterson practiced six hours or more a day. In 1940, he won a talent competition sponsored by the Canadian Broadcasting Corporation. Soon after, he began working professionally.

Peterson was one of the most virtuosic of jazz pianists. Major influences were Teddy Wilson, Nat "King" Cole and, particularly, Art Tatum. In his playing, OP effectively deployed an arsenal of effects: cascading streams of notes as dazzling as the tail of a comet, displays of breath-taking bravura, strong chordal passages reminiscent of Harlem stride, and episodes of subtle, spacious lyricism. Oscar was also a skilled and sensitive accompanist, never overwhelming the many artists he backed, including Benny Carter, Coleman Hawkins, Ben Webster, Stan Getz, and Ella Fitzgerald.

Peterson came to the attention of jazz impresario and producer Norman Granz in 1947, the beginning of an association that spanned much of OP's career. He featured on Granz's well-known Jazz at the Philharmonic tours and signed with his Verve label, where he became the house pianist. This exposure, plus his frenetic touring and recording schedule, made Oscar one of the best-known performers in jazz.

Peterson worked almost exclusively with a trio. The classic 1950s version consisted of guitarist Herb Ellis and bassist Ray Brown. Ellis was replaced by drummer Ed Thigpen in 1959; in 1965 bassist Sam Jones and drummer Louis Hayes became the rhythm section. The bass and drums laid down a rollicking rhythm which Oscar top-coated with his quicksilver phrases. On his best recordings, he knew exactly when to put his foot to the floor and when to move into the slow lane.

A favourite formula of Granz's was to make albums of the work of the great American songwriters. OP went at it with a vengeance in the 1950s, recording the music of Irving Berlin, George Gershwin, Cole Porter, Jerome Kern, Richard Rodgers, Harold Arlen and others. In 1996, Verve creamed off the highlights on a two CD set, *The Song Is You*. In his liner notes, Richard Palmer (who collaborated with Peterson on his autobiography, *A Jazz Odyssey*) has described the playing as

> delicate thoughtful and invigorating; the musicians display a near infallible feel for dynamics and tempo. The accent is on the American popular song at its best. Even in the development section the musicians never stray very far from the melody, and while the harmonies are often recast imaginatively, the songs' essential properties are always discernible.

Two of Peterson's most popular LPs in the 1960s were *Night Train* and *We Get Requests*. I've never found either entirely satisfactory: the former has too much finger busting for the sake of it and the latter is so cool it veers towards cocktail jazz. More enjoyable is *The London House Sessions*, uniformly high-quality live performances recorded in Chicago in 1961 and released in their entirety as a five CD set in 1996.

The height of OP's achievement was the series of recordings he made from 1963-68 for Hans Georg Brunner-Schwer's MPS label, released on four CDs as *Exclusively for My Friends*. Brunner-Schwer had become friendly with Oscar and invited him to record at his luxurious villa at Villingen in the Black Forest before a small, invited audience. The occasion was so successful that it became the first of a series. Rarely have Oscar's opulent effusions been so well captured and rarely has he sounded so relaxed and thoughtful. The music ranges across every facet of his style, from introspective, melodic musings to swinging, propulsive blues.

One of the Villingen LPs, *My Favourite Instrument*, was Oscar's first solo record. He made another for MPS in 1970, *Tracks*. Gene Lees (who wrote a biography of Peterson, *The Will to Swing*) has described it as

> an even greater masterpiece than the first. The album is fairly evenly divided between driving, powerful, up-tempo performances and ballad playing. One might say it represents the two sides of Oscar's psyche: one of them exuberant, joyous, witty, and utterly confident; the other pensive, brooding exploratory, and touched with a melancholy he refuses to surrender to.

Regrettably and inexplicably, Peterson released only one other solo record, consisting of live performances from 1972 in Lebanon and Amsterdam.

In the 1970s, OP often worked with bassist Niels-Henning Ørsted Pedersen and guitarist Joe Pass. In 1975, Peterson recorded *À La Salle Pleyel* live with Pass. Both perform solo sets then come together for a duo bracket. I was fortunate enough to hear them at about that time at the Sydney Opera House. I can still vividly recall the intensity and energy of Oscar's performance, the sweat pouring off him and the inspiration flowing out of him.

Oscar's lifestyle indulgences – tobacco, food, and wives (he was married four times) – were not as destructive as those of many of his jazz colleagues. His personal decency and generosity of spirit are illustrated by his support of the ill-starred pianist Hampton Hawes. In his autobiography, Hawes recalled:

> Every so often I'd raise the piano lid on opening night and there'd be a telegram: 'Best wishes for a successful opening and successful engagement – Oscar Peterson and the Trio'. The club owners would tell me, Oscar gave a speech about you,

told them to be sure and come back next week to hear you. A good brother taking care of his own (Hampton Hawes with Don Asher, Raise up off Me: a portrait of Hampton Hawes, Coward, McCann and Geoghegan, 1974).

In the 1980s Oscar battled arthritis in his hands and had a severe stroke in 1993. He gradually taught himself to play again and became almost as busy as ever. Oscar Peterson died of kidney failure on 23 December 2007.

37. "BUD" POWELL (1924-1966)

As Charlie Parker was to the bebop saxophone, "Bud" Powell was to the piano. He had a virtuosic technique, as good as Art Tatum, although he pioneered a linear style, without the left hand beating out the rhythm as the Harlem stride pianists did. Bud did make good use of his left hand, but it was not a predominant element of his playing. As well as being unsurpassed for speed and articulation, Powell played ballads with opulent, orchestral chords. Almost every jazz pianist since has drawn on his legacy. Bud's work had a dark, disturbing side. According to critic Gary Giddins: "The surface of his music seems frequently to be a mask made up of bebop acrobatics, convoluted triplets and flashy chromatic runs. Lurking below, however, is a confluence of emotions, ranging from self-lacerating ferocity to an elegant benignity".

Earl Rudolph Powell was born in Harlem on 27 September 1924. His father was a jazz pianist and Bud began piano lessons at age five. A prodigy, he began playing jazz professionally in his mid-teens. Powell impressed Thelonious Monk, whose protégé he became. Monk introduced him to the burgeoning New York bebop scene.

Powell had severe mental health issues, not helped by his alcoholism. As well as being a chronic drunk, he was a chronic smart-ass, not a good idea for a black man in the racist USA. Powell's out-of-control lip when he had been drinking led him into numerous altercations. In 1945, he was severely beaten by police, leading to the first of many incarcerations in mental institutions.

From 1949-51, Powell recorded for Norman Granz's Verve label. On *Jazz Giant*, a 1949 trio LP, Powell plays superbly but unfortunately the poor quality of the recording does not capture his lustrous sound well. In February 1951, Bud recorded a solo session featuring five of his compositions. It is the indispensable Powell, combining speed of light runs with musical sensibility. "A Nightingale Sang in Berkeley Square" is a miniature masterpiece, skilfully blending bop dexterity, stride piano and lush romanticism.

The Amazing Bud Powell Volumes One and Two on Blue Note capture Bud at his peak. The first session from 1949 features Powell with the cream of bop musicians: trumpeter "Fats" Navarro, "Sonny" Rollins on tenor, Tommy Potter on bass and drummer Roy Haynes. The second CD is from 1953 with George Duvivier on bass and Art Taylor on drums, Bud's usual rhythm section for the next four years. It features three takes of "Autumn in New York", some of the most emotive jazz piano ever recorded. Also included is the definitive version of what many consider Powell's most significant composition, "Glass Enclosure". The title refers to an apartment in which Bud was kept under virtual house arrest to ensure he turned up in good shape for an engagement at jazz club Birdland. *Strictly Powell* and *Swingin' with Bud* are trio recordings from 1956-57. Rather than the red-hot flames of the past, Bud's playing is more glowing embers, but some of the old magic is still there.

From the mid-1950s, Powell's mental health deteriorated dramatically. He became notorious for unreliability and unpredictability and the quality of his playing declined. The inventor of bop piano often sounded like just another bop pianist. A partial exception is *Portrait of Thelonious* from 1961 in which Bud pays tribute to his old mentor. Powell moved to Paris in 1959. He became friendly with a young admirer, Francis Paudras, who tried to help him get his life together, with varying degrees of success. Paudras wrote a book about his experiences with Powell which became the basis of the movie *'Round Midnight*, starring Dexter Gordon whose own life had something in common with Powell's.

In 1963, Powell returned to New York for a disastrous attempt at a comeback. He died of cirrhosis, tuberculosis and malnutrition on 31 July 1966 at the age of 41.

38. IKE QUEBEC (1918-1963)

I have a weakness for the robust, bluesy tenor saxophone players of the Swing era – tough guys on the surface but real softies
when it came to a ballad. As well as the duumvirate of Coleman
Hawkins and Ben Webster, there were a lot of strong contenders
in the second division: Don Byas, "Lockjaw" Davis, "Bud" Johnson, "Buddy" Tate, and, a personal favourite, Ike Quebec. While
Ike could effortlessly produce those dark, rich notes so characteristic of the tenor, he had a lighter sound than many, with a hint of
acerbity in the upper register. The *Penguin Guide to Jazz* (8th ed)
has commented that Quebec had "a beautiful, sinuous tone and an
innate melodic sense, negotiating standards with a simplicity and
lack of arrogance that are refreshing and even therapeutic".

Ike Abrams Quebec was born in Newark, New Jersey on 17 August 1918. After an early career as a dancer and pianist, he switched to tenor in 1940. Ike played with many of the big names of the Swing era: Benny Carter, Roy Eldridge, Coleman Hawkins. From 1944-51 he was with "Cab" Calloway's band.

When Swing and the big bands went out of fashion in the 1950s, Quebec had a tough time, not helped by his heroin habit. He worked for Alfred Lion of the Blue Note label as a talent scout, arranger, and organiser of innumerable sessions. Lion was an admirer of Ike's playing and decided to re-launch his career in 1959. Jazz writer Ira Gitler whimsically announced his return: "Montreal may be in Quebec, but Quebec is in New York and Blue Note's got him. Ike's got rhythm. Who could ask for anything more?" To re-familiarise the audience with Ike, Lion decided on a series of singles aimed at the still-flourishing juke box market. It was the sort of music the patrons of Harlem bars wanted to hear in those days – a stark contrast to the mind-numbing monotony of rap – and they sold well. The complete 45 rpm recordings were reissued on CD in 2005, two hours of excellent mainstream tenor playing.

Quebec went on to cut a series of memorable LPs for Blue Note. His playing retained all its old virtues but had a new maturity and sensibility. *Heavy Soul* is marred by the presence of organist Freddie Roach but he is less obtrusive on *It Might as Well be Spring* which has some sumptuous ballads. *Soul Samba* is Quebec's entry in the bossa nova stakes. With Kenny Burrell on guitar, it is only a nose behind the heavily-favoured *Jazz Samba* from the Stan Getz/Charlie Byrd stable. In 1997, Blue Note issued *Ballads*, a late-night compilation featuring Ike at his mellow best.

In December 1961, Quebec recorded two masterpieces. *Born to be Blue* was released under the name of guitarist Grant Green, another whose life and career were marred by heroin addiction. Green played seemingly endless, virtuosic single note solos and, like Ike, is in peak form. On *Blue and Sentimental* Ike has a superior supporting cast: Miles Davis' rhythm section of Paul Chambers and "Philly" Joe Jones, plus Green. Critic Roy Carr has said that the album "lives up to its title as, with a stylish flourish, Ike wantonly cuts across current fashions for a spot of unashamed heart-string tugging".

Ike Quebec's renaissance was cut tragically short. He died of lung cancer on 16 January 1963 at the age of 44. Saxophonist Johnny Griffin recalled: "When Ike died they closed all the clubs for the night, and I think just about everyone who was there followed his coffin".

39. "DJANGO" REINHARDT (1910-1953)

The only non-American to appear in this book is French Gypsy guitarist "Django" Reinhardt. He is a major soloist in anyone's terms. Without formal tuition and having a deformed left hand, Django created endless virtuosic single note improvisations in any key and tempo. He was a peerless rhythm player who dominated every group he was in with his instantly recognisable swing. Django's solos have a ringing, steely clarity, yet also a soulful resonance. His Romany heritage gave his music a unique flavour.

Jean Reinhardt was born on 23 January 1910 at a Gypsy encampment at Liberchies, Pont-à-Celles, Belgium. He showed early musical aptitude, playing the violin and then guitar. By 15 he was making a living busking in Paris, often working with his brother Joseph, also an accomplished guitarist. In November 1928, the caravan Django and his wife were living in caught fire. He was severely burnt, taking 18 months to recover. According to Django's biographer, Michael Dregni, his left hand was "a clawed hook, the back shrunken into a knot of scars. His two small fingers were largely paralysed". Slowly, he taught himself to perform again, finding new ways to play notes and chords (*Django: the life and music of a Gypsy legend*, OUP, 2004).

In 1931, Django heard recordings of Louis Armstrong and "Duke" Ellington and was hooked on jazz. Soon after, he met jazz violinist and occasional pianist Stephane Grappelli, who proved to be a compatible musical – if not personal – partner. Although he had briefly studied music formally, Grappelli was also largely self-taught and had been a street musician. His fluent, melodious lines complemented Django's more percussive sound. The two jammed together and then formed a group, the Quintette du Hot Club de France. The other original members were Django's brother Joseph and Roger Chaput on guitars plus Louis Vola on bass.

An all-string group was unusual but with the guitars laying down the rhythm it swung as hard as any band with a drummer. According to Dregni, their rhythmic style was known as "the pump" because of its fierce up and down beat. It was an ideal foundation for Django's solos: "His two fingers pranced through precise chromatic runs, flourishes of diminished arpeggios and minor seventh scales, hit intriguing intervals, proudly unveiling his trademark riffs, turning the song inside out" (*Django: the life and music of a Gypsy legend*, OUP, 2004).

The Hot Club was an immediate success and made Django a star. Between 1934 and the outbreak of World War Two, the group produced a succession of classic recordings. Behind the scenes, things were less than harmonious. Django was vain, self-indulgent and irresponsible. He would demand unrealistic fees, miss performances, turn up without a guitar, and throw a tantrum if he felt he had been slighted. The sombre, serious Grappelli, who often had to deal with the consequences, was infuriated by his colleague's feckless behaviour. On New Year's Eve in 1937, a fight between Django and his long-suffering brother Joseph landed both in gaol.

British critic Charles Fox has observed that for American jazz musicians who visited Paris in the second half of the 1930s "it was almost as obligatory to record – or sit in with – Reinhardt as to inspect Versailles or take the lift up the Eiffel Tower". The stand-out recording session was with Coleman Hawkins and Benny Carter in April 1937. There were also some excellent duo performances with violinist Eddie South later that year. In 1939, visiting Ellingtonians Rex Stewart and Barney Bigard recorded with Django, proving that, as Fox says, it was possible for "at least one European to operate on the same level as the finest American players" (M Harrison, C Fox and E Thacker, *The Essential Jazz Records: ragtime to swing*, Da Capo, 1988).

Grappelli spent the war years in London, working with blind pianist George Shearing. After decades of neglect he bounced back in the 1970s, recording and touring prolifically. Stephane worked with musicians as diverse as Gary Burton, Earl Hines, Yehudi Menuhin, Oscar Peterson and McCoy Tyner. His most successful group was the Hot Club of London which returned to the all-string format, with two guitars and bass. This outfit's finest recording is *Live in London* from 1973, with Grappelli playing at his peak. I had the privilege of hearing them at Sydney Town Hall and will never forget their swinging version of "The Road to Gundagai". Stephane was still working when he died on 1 December 1997 at the age of 89.

Django continued to perform in occupied France, despite the Nazis' persecution of Gypsies, and remained immensely popular. He and Grappelli reunited periodically after the war but much of the old spark was gone, an exception being a session in London in early 1946 which produced "Echoes of France", a version of "La Marseillaise".

In 1946, Django accepted an invitation from Duke Ellington to perform in the US. Duke featured him on an extensive tour. Ellington, the audiences, fellow guitarists, and many critics were dazzled by his virtuosity. On the other hand, Django turned up so late for a performance at Carnegie Hall that Duke had already announced he would not be appearing. Reinhardt felt uncomfortable in America and increasingly yearned for his homeland. In February 1947, he returned to France, disillusioned and convinced that the trip had been a failure (*Django: the life and music of a Gypsy legend*, OUP, 2004).

It is a tribute to Django's genius that he completely mastered the electric guitar. Lacking the fiendish energy of the 1930s, though not the dexterity, his playing was silkier, warmer, almost wistful at times. The sessions produced by Eddie Barclay (aka Edouard Roualt) for his Blue Star label between 1947 and 1953 are the best example of Django's later style. He used a conventional rhythm section and was accompanied on many tracks by long-time collaborator clarinettist Hubert Rostaing, a talented player in the Benny Goodman tradition. Django was still capable of producing a near-perfect solo, and many believe the 10 March 1953 version of "Nuages", his most famous composition, is the finest.

Django's reputation had faded by the 1950s and he worked only intermittently. He spent much time in the small village of Samois-sur-Seine on the outskirts of Paris, fishing and socialising in the local cafés. It was here that Django died of a cerebral haemorrhage on 16 May 1953 aged 43.

40. "SONNY" ROLLINS (1930 –)

The main stylistic alternative in the New York hard bop scene to tenor saxophonist John Coltrane was "Sonny" Rollins. He was a staccato soloist who preferred choppy phrases to the long, surging lines Coltrane favoured. Rollins was a quirky player who could be whimsical, even satirical if the mood took him. On other occasions he played with diabolical energy. His tone was often plangent, almost grating, although he could sometimes sound richly sonorous. Rollins never aspired to the transcendent and spiritual as Coltrane did, basing his music in a visceral earthiness. His usual approach resembled a lion clawing at the bars of his cage. Rollins is a paradoxical, inconsistent musician – at his best a giant, at other times almost a caricature of himself.

Walter Theodore Rollins was born on 7 September 1930 in New York. He was a prodigy, playing saxophone from an early age and becoming a professional after graduating from high school in 1948. He worked with many of the bebop giants such as Charlie Parker, Thelonious Monk and Miles Davis. Sonny was a member of the legendary Clifford Brown-Max Roach Quintet until its short existence ended with the deaths of Brown and pianist Richie Powell in a car accident in 1956. Like many others, Rollins succumbed to the occupational hazard of heroin addiction, serving time in gaol before kicking his habit in the mid-1950s.

As a leader, Rollins exploded on the scene like a supernova. In 1956-57, he recorded almost a dozen LPs. It was *Tenor Madness*, as his 1956 LP is entitled. *Saxophone Colossus* (1956) is the masterpiece from this period, containing Sonny's most famous composition, the calypso "St Thomas", and the ground-breaking "Blue Seven". More relaxed is an April 1957 session for Blue Note, *Sonny Rollins Volume Two*, with Thelonious Monk on two tracks. It concludes with one of Sonny's most beautiful ballad performances, "Poor Butterfly". *Newk's Time* from September 1957 is another tour de force. In November 1957, Rollins recorded *Live at the Village Vanguard*, reissued in its entirety on two CDs in 1999. Accompanied only by bass and drums, he is like a tunnel-boring machine, inexorably grinding up all in front of him. The result is powerful but relentlessly austere, and the absence of a piano adds to the bleakness.

In 1959, when he was one of the most acclaimed musicians in jazz, Rollins took the first of a number of extended sabbaticals. At night he practised regularly and relentlessly on the Williamsburg Bridge in New York. Ornette Coleman and free jazz became the new fashion during this time. Some assumed Rollins was experimenting with innovative ideas; in fact, he was perfecting his technique.

Sonny's 1962 come-back album, *The Bridge*, was decidedly conventional in approach, featuring guitarist Jim Hall, who was mainly associated with west coast jazz. Rollins was at his peak, playing with freshness and vitality. The follow-up, *What's New*, was more mixed but had some classic tracks such as "If Ever I would Leave You" and "The Night Has a Thousand Eyes". Hall has reminisced:

> I can't really say why he chose me to be in the group, although it was very flattering, especially when I realised what I had gotten into. The standards were extremely high – and he set such a high standard himself, in his playing and on and off the stand. He was just marvellous to work with.

In the mid-1960s, Rollins recorded two lesser known but enjoyable albums, *On Impulse* and *Alfie*, the latter based on music he had composed for the film. After another period of retirement, *Next Album* from 1972, featuring the excellent pianist George Cables, was surprisingly mellow. The highlight is "Skylark" with its lengthy unaccompanied opening and closing passages.

Rollins had a long, prolific, idiosyncratic career, still performing and recording in his 80s. He finally gave up playing in 2014 for health reasons. Pete King, saxophonist and co-proprietor of famous London jazz club Ronnie Scott's, said that Rollins could play a tune "any way he felt like, upside down, backwards, inside out, and it would be up to the guys in the rhythm section to get it – he'd never hand out any music. Amazing improvising musician, amazing human being".

41. ARTIE SHAW (1910-2004)

The main contender for Benny Goodman's crown as king of swing was fellow clarinettist Artie Shaw. Both led superlative, swinging big bands, featuring propulsive, showman drummers, Gene Krupa and "Buddy" Rich respectively. In terms of technique, honours were about even, although Shaw had the smoother tone, as mellow as an aged malt whisky. Musically, Artie was more innovative than Benny, who preferred to stick to his established formula. Personally, both were perfectionists who were notoriously temperamental and difficult to work with.

Shaw had a richer hinterland compared to the rather monochromatic Goodman. According to Artie: "I played music, Goodman played the clarinet. All he ever wanted to talk about was the damn instrument" (*New York Times*, 18 August 1994). Shaw published a well-regarded autobiography in 1952, *The Trouble with Cinderella*, and subsequently wrote novels and short stories. He was skilled at higher mathematics and was an expert marksman and fly fisherman.

Arthur Jacob Arshawsky was born on 23 May 1910 in Manhattan's Lower East Side, the only child of poor Jewish immigrants. He taught himself to play saxophone, then clarinet, and to read and arrange music. As a teenager, Artie played with local bands and soon graduated to being a professional. He worked with popular Swing band leaders and was a much sought-after session musician.

Having been the victim of anti-semitic taunts as a child, he changed his surname to Shaw when he was 20. In spite of this, jazz pianist and historian Tony Baldwin has noted that there is

> a degree of (possibly unconscious) Klezmer/Jewish influence on Shaw's playing, discernible in the various recordings of 'Softly, as in a Morning Sunrise', 'The Chant', 'Dr Livingstone I Presume', and 'Concerto for Clarinet'. In a similar but less obvious way, I find there is a kind of *mitteleuropäisch* mood about some of the 1936 recordings, particularly 'Sweet Lorraine', where Artie achieves a knife-edge balance between the quasi-Viennese schmaltz of the fiddles, the drive of the swinging guitar and his own muscular lyricism (email to the author).

In 1936, Shaw tried his luck as a leader but with little commercial success initially. His first band, with a string section, did record one memorable piece, "Streamline", a virtuoso showcase for Artie. Two years later, an engagement with a new band at the Roseland Ballroom, which was broadcast nation-wide, brought him fame and a recording contract with RCA. Live recordings from the Café Rouge and Blue Room in New York in 1938-39 capture this great outfit in its prime. The superbly swinging "Carioca" demonstrates why readers of Downbeat voted Shaw's orchestra the number one band of 1938.

Artie's first studio recording session for RCA in July 1938 produced a number one hit, "Begin the Beguine", still his most famous record. Other notable recordings from this period are "Deep Purple" (with a slinky vocal by Helen Forrest), "Deep in a Dream", the eerie "Nightmare" (Shaw's theme song), and "Any Old Time" with Billie Holiday.

Artie commented that his band's arrangements – many by Jerry Gray who went on to become a mainstay of Glenn Miller's orchestra – had "crystal clear transparency. The arrangement itself was simple, essentially; as a result even a lay listener could see all the way through to the bottom, as when you look into a clear pool of water, and see the band at the bottom of the pool".

Shaw had a troubled, tumultuous personality. In 1939, he disparaged his fans as morons, walked out on the band, and headed off to Acapulco for a sabbatical. Even then Artie could not remain anonymous – he rescued a drowning woman and subsequent press reports blew his cover. There were similar episodes of retreating into seclusion throughout his career. A *New York Times* profile observed that Shaw had two personas: "One, a reclusive intellectual, a bookworm and a writer, uneasy with crowds and bored with celebrity; the other 'Artie Shaw, the clarinet player who married all those chicks." (Frank Prial, 18 August 1994). Shaw was married eight times, including to Lana Turner and Ava Gardner. His ex-wives described him as obsessively controlling and abusive.

Inspired by music he had heard during his Mexican sojourn, Shaw returned to the studio in March 1940 and cut "Frenesi", a symphonic master work in microcosm which sold over a million copies. His follow-up recordings, with a band featuring a nine-piece string section, were just as good, including "Georgia", "Stardust" and "Concerto for Clarinet". The last has become a standard work. I remember being surprised when one of my daughter's fellow music students played it for her final year high school recital.

Artie was at the summit of success in the 1940s. With his movie-star good looks, celebrity marriages, and a succession of hits the money was rolling in: "Thirty, forty, fifty thousand a week. I decided to live like no emperor had ever lived – and I did" (*New York Times*, 18 August 1994).

In 1942, Shaw joined the Navy and led a band which toured the Pacific for 18 months, coming under Japanese fire a number of times. When lead tenor saxophonist Sam Donahue came down with fever, one of Australia's greatest jazz musicians, Merv Acheson, was sent by the Army to replace him. Merv told me that the charts had been so damaged by constant exposure to the elements that he found them very hard to read. The other difficulty he had was Shaw, whom he admired musically but found to be an unpleasant person.

Like Goodman, Shaw had a small unit he recorded with, the Gramercy Five, named after his New York phone number. The first sessions in 1940 featured trumpeter Billy Butterfield and Johnny Guarnieri on harpsichord. Rather than being incongruous, the harpsichord added a percussive complement to Shaw's mellifluous solos. "Summit Ridge Drive", "My Blue Heaven" and "Smoke Gets in your Eyes" are classic chamber jazz performances. The 1945 version of the Gramercy Five featured Roy Eldridge on trumpet. Like Goodman, Shaw was a pioneer of racially integrated bands. Unfortunately, it cut only half a dozen tracks. Artie formed his final version of the Gramercy Five in 1953. Although it is now virtually forgotten, this outfit, which included pianist Hank Jones and guitarist Tal Farlow, recorded some of his best music. Shaw's virtuosity and swing were as evident as ever but now had a reflective maturity.

In 1954, Artie retired from performing. "I did all I could with the clarinet", he said, "any more would have been less". He described leaving the music business as like "cutting off a gangrenous arm. You miss it but better to have one arm and have a life" (*New York Times*, 18 August 1994). Artie Shaw died on 30 December 2004 aged 94.

42. ART TATUM (1909-56)

Art Tatum is one of the greatest of jazz musicians, with technical and improvisatory skills on the level of Louis Armstrong and Charlie Parker. This was in spite of the fact that he was blind in one eye and had very little sight in the other. Art consumed enormous quantities of alcohol but it never affected his playing. Some have criticised his pianism as overly ornate, with the technical skill overwhelming the music. To me, Tatum plays with a rococo beauty, his improvisations elegantly enhancing and elucidating the melody without engulfing it.

Tatum re-invented the Harlem stride piano style of James P Johnson and "Fats" Waller, "pushing it harmonically, polyphonically and pianistically beyond anything imagined". Legendary classical pianist Vladimir Horowitz was "inspired and intimidated by the inventiveness and sheer virtuosity of Tatum's playing: the intricate rhythmic riffs, the constantly shifting harmony, the hyper-charged keyboard-sweeping runs". Other piano virtuosi, such as Sergei Rachmaninoff, Walter Gieseking and Arthur Rubinstein, were Tatum admirers (Anthony Tommasini, *New York Times*, 21 July 2006).

Arthur Tatum Jr was born in Toledo, Ohio, on 13 October 1909. Neither of his parents were musical but they were religious and Art was influenced by the music he heard in church as a child. A prodigy with perfect pitch, he taught himself to play, although he also had some formal tuition at school. In his teens he was working professionally and had his own radio show which was broadcast nationally.

Moving to New York in the 1930s, Tatum built a huge reputation. He was in demand at the top clubs, usually working solo – partly because few other musicians could keep up with him. When he finished, he would often move on to smaller after-hours joints, sometimes playing until dawn. When Tatum walked into a club where Waller was working, "Fats" announced: "Ladies and gentlemen, I play piano, but tonight God is in the house". By the mid-1940s, Tatum had moved from the clubs to the concert halls, with equal success.

From 1934-40 Tatum made a series of classic solo recordings for Decca. His playing is intense, inventive and invigorating. Tatum recorded for Capitol from 1949-52. As well as the solo tracks, there are some trio sides with guitarist Everett Barksdale and, unfortunately, bassist "Slam" Stewart. The latter's trademark was humming along with his bowed solos, one of the most excruciating sounds jazz has produced – until free jazz came along anyway.

There is a sense of marking time about this period – not bad, but not great.

Tatum was recorded a number of times in informal settings. Two sets stand out for musical and acoustic quality: *In Private* from 1948 and *Twentieth Century Piano Genius*. The latter was recorded in 1950 and 1955 at parties at the Beverly Hills home of Ray Heindorf, musical director for Warner Brothers. In those days the A list had taste. Art's playing is relaxed but rivetting.

Tatum's finest music resulted from his association with jazz impresario Norman Granz from 1953-56. Granz got Tatum into the studio, sat him down at the piano, turned on the tape, and told him to play. When re-issued on CD, the results comfortably filled eight discs. It is a pinnacle of jazz achievement. Tatum plays his usual repertoire of standards and show tunes in a mellow, magisterial way. Critic and jazz musician Benny Green, who wrote perceptive liner notes for the series, says that it was a marathon for which Tatum had "inadvertently been preparing all his life, for Tatum's repertoire was as stupefying as the art he brought to it. Tatum is the greatest jazz pianist of all time, the songs he chose the greatest of a much maligned but nonetheless sublime repertoire. That is why these performances are immortal".

Granz also recorded eight CDs of Tatum group performances with the cream of contemporary musicians. Some don't come off but others are undoubted masterpieces which definitively disprove the canard that Tatum could not work with a band – though playing a solo after him was not for the faint-hearted. In June 1954, Tatum recorded a sparkling album with the inimitable Benny Carter on alto sax and Louis Bellson on drums. There was an excellent follow-up session, with an unusually restrained Roy Eldridge on trumpet.

While some responded to Tatum's flourishes by trying to match him, "Little Jazz" wisely pared down his style to a subdued splendour. A trio date in January 1956 with Jo Jones on drums and bassist Red Callender yielded some magisterial small group jazz.

Next month, Art was in the studio with an unlikely but compatible partner, Buddy DeFranco, who had the misfortune to be playing clarinet when it went out of fashion in the bebop era. DeFranco was one of the few musicians whose technical facility matched that of Tatum. In an interview in 2009, he said that Tatum "went after me with both barrels. It wasn't a nasty thing. It was a game. An enjoyable game. It also allowed us to get into the music thoroughly". He recalled that "Art was a lot of fun. He laughed a lot. I remember he drank more beer on that date than I could imagine. Once in a while he took a shot of gin. But the effects never showed" (Marc Myers, *JazzWax*, https://www.jazzwax.com/2009/04/interview-buddy-de-franco-on-tatum.html).

A particularly enjoyable session is that of September 1956 with Ben Webster. His big, brooding tenor sax hovers above Tatum's swift-flowing piano like a swan flapping its wings. Sadly, it was Tatum's swan song. He died of kidney failure on 5 November 1956 aged 47.

43. JACK TEAGARDEN (1905-64)

The trombone, I have to admit, is not my favourite jazz instrument. Too often, its exponents produce a blaring, blasting sound that soon grates on the ear. There are a few exceptions: JJ Johnson in the bebop era, long-time Ellingtonian Lawrence Brown, and, above all, Jack Teagarden.

"Big T" had a broad, languid sound that was rich and smooth as molasses. His improvisations were agile for his cumbersome instrument, effortlessly swinging, endlessly inventive, and saturated in the blues. He was also one of the greatest jazz vocalists, with a deep-hued, husky voice redolent of thousands of nights of cheap booze and cigarettes in smoke-filled bars.

Weldon Leo "Jack" Teagarden was born in Vernon, Texas, on 20 August 1905 and raised in Tennessee. His father was an amateur cornetist and his mother taught piano. Jack's brother Charlie was a trumpeter in the Armstrong tradition and his sister Norma a jazz pianist. Largely self-taught, Teagarden was playing trombone at age seven and working professionally from 1921.

In 1927, "Big T" arrived in New York. Ben Pollack, who led one of the top white bands of the day, soon recruited him. A classic Teagarden performance with Pollack is "My Kind of Love" from 1929. Jack was with Paul Whiteman's prestigious but pretentious orchestra from 1934-38. He also worked with top New York musicians such as "Red" Nichols and Joe Venuti.

In New York, Jack became friendly with Benny Goodman, Gene Krupa, "Bud" Freeman, Eddie Condon and other musicians of the Chicago school. Jazz scholar Dan Morgenstern has noted that what distinguished their music was a rhythmic drive that "took its cues from the jazz of Chicago's south side; a much hotter brand of black music than what was heard in Harlem or downtown Manhattan". Teagarden fitted in perfectly and made some memorable recordings with the Chicagoans, for example, "Basin Street Blues" and "Beale Street Blues" in 1928, and in the following year "I'm Going to Stomp Mr Henry Lee" and "That's a Serious Thing".

In 1939, Jack formed his own big band. It was an accomplished outfit which made some fine records such as "A Hundred Years from Today", "Octoroon" and "Swingin' on the Teagarden Gate". However, the hard-drinking, easy-going Teagarden was temperamentally unsuited to the day-to-day necessities of running a band and it was a financial disaster.

In 1947, Jack joined Louis Armstrong for a productive four years. They were personally and musically well-matched, inspiring each other to ever greater heights, from the jocular banter of "Rockin' Chair" to the sublime beauty of "St James' Infirmary". A concert at Symphony Hall in Boston in November 1947 captures the All Stars at their peak. "Big T" rarely played or sang better than on "Stars Fell on Alabama" and his virtuosity on "Baby won't you Please Come Home" and "Lover" is astonishing.

For the rest of his life, Jack worked with small combos. His finest late record as leader is *Meet Me Where They Play the Blues* from 1954. Sympathetically supervised by Leonard Feather, it featured an all-star line-up: Jimmy McPartland on cornet, Ed Hall on clarinet, Dick Cary on piano and trumpet, and Walter Page on bass. The title track has a beguiling, easy swing and Jack infuses the lyrics with a world-weary melancholy:

> Eyes that flirt with a tear are common 'round here. Misery loves company, they say. So I linger 'til dawn while the trumpet wails on hopin' you'll happen this way. I'm getting' tired of sippin' wine and watchin' it bubble. How did our dreams get out of line and wind up in trouble?

Teagarden often re-united with the old Chicago gang. In 1957 he featured on a Bud Freeman revival LP, *Chicago/Austin High School Jazz in Hi-Fi*, stealing the show with his poignant performance on "I Cover the Waterfront". A fruitful partnership was with cornetist Bobby Hackett. *The Coast Concert* (1955) and *Jazz Ultimate* (1958) showcase Teagarden at his ebullient, effervescent best. A highlight of *The Coast Concert* is "Basin Street Blues" which concludes magisterially with Jack announcing: "Look out folks, I'm going to take a trambone [sic] coda".

Nothing in life mattered as much to Teagarden as his music and he spent most of his time on the road. He had a customised trombone case that had room for a radio, a clean shirt, a bottle of whisky and other home comforts. Jack's friend, journalist Tony Weitzel, recalled:

> He was a nervous guy, never quite comfortable sitting down or standing still. I asked him a couple of years ago when he was playing in Chicago if he ever felt really peaceful. Jack said, 'When I blow a big noise out of that old horn, then I feel peaceful. I guess that's the only time' (*Chicago Daily News*, 17 January 1964).

In Teagarden's final years, alcoholism took its toll. *On Mis'ry and the Blues*, recorded in 1961, his powers are obviously waning. Jack Teagarden died alone in a hotel room in New Orleans of a heart attack complicated by pneumonia on 15 January 1964 aged 58.

44. JOE VENUTI (1903-78)

Jazz has produced few violinists who are major soloists. The first and greatest was Joe Venuti, a major influence on those who came after him, such as Eddie South, "Stuff" Smith and Stephane Grappelli.

Giuseppe Venuti was born in Philadelphia on 16 September 1903 of Italian parents and trained as a classical violinist. He was also a competent pianist and guitarist. In the mid-1920s, Venuti moved to New York. It was there that he reunited with an old school friend, Eddie Lang, born Salvatore Massaro, the first significant white jazz guitarist. Eddie recorded with legendary New Orleans cornetist "King" Oliver (under the pseudonym "Blind Willie Dunn"), blues guitarist Lonnie Johnson, Bessie Smith, and was "Bing" Crosby's favourite accompanist. Critic Vic Bellerby has astutely observed that Venuti and Lang "had no jazz tradition, no basic soil or subsoil on which their musical plants could thrive. They originated a standard of rhythmic progression, personal tone and unique phrasing which was to influence every jazz guitarist and violinist in the future". The roots they drew on were European.

Joe and Eddie's late 1920s duets, such as "Stringing the Blues", "Four String Joe" and "Wild Cat", are amongst the finest chamber jazz ever recorded. Just as good are a series of small group recordings made at the same time with top New York musicians, including Adrian Rollini, Frankie Trumbauer and Jimmy Dorsey. Highlights are "A Mug of Ale", "Dinah", "I'll Never be the Same", and "Little Girl" (with a swinging vocal by songwriter Harold Arlen). Venuti and Lang's music has been described as

> always witty and inventive, and rhythmically most relaxed, with Lang inclined to lie back on the beat rather than push it. In the duets it is Venuti who takes the dominant role, his playing full of devices that catch the attention. Lang was content to be an accompanist yet one of such brilliance that the listener can find satisfaction just contemplating his use of harmony, his skill at providing rhythmic impetus (Charles Fox in M Harrison, C Fox and E Thacker, *The Essential Jazz Records: ragtime to swing*, Da Capo, 1988).

The peak of Venuti and Lang's achievement was a recording date on 29 October 1931 with Jack and Charlie Teagarden and Benny Goodman. It produced four classic tracks: "Beale Street Blues", "After You've Gone", "Someday Sweetheart", and "Farewell Blues". Jazz scholar Dan Morgenstern has said that this session "in its totality achieves some kind of near perfection of collective empathy".

Lang died of a botched tonsillectomy in 1933. Venuti's career languished in the post-war decades as jazz fashions changed and his alcoholism took an increasing toll.

Joe had a renaissance in the 1970s, when he recorded for Hank O'Neal's Chiaroscuro label. Hank described Venuti as "one of a kind, a larger-than-life figure who would happily bash a tormentor or scold a musician for a flawed performance. He wouldn't tolerate fools but was kind to children and dogs. He also made great music and was one of the merriest people I ever met".

O'Neal recorded Joe in a variety of small group settings, including with that most swinging of tenor sax players, "Zoot" Sims, and the exhibitionist of the keyboard, Earl Hines. Venuti had matured to new levels of virtuosity and sensibility. His playing was "coloured by unexpected bursts of pizzicato, oddball kinds of bowing and resinous streams of melody that seem to go on forever" (*Penguin Guide to Jazz*, 6th ed).

The final masterpiece was *Alone at the Palace* recorded in April 1977 with Dave McKenna on piano. Joe is at his most poignant on the ballads and swings harder than ever on the cookers. "Big Dave" complements him perfectly at both tempos. Particularly enjoyable is Joe singing his composition "Ain't Doin' Bad Doin' Nothin". The lyrics really resonated when I retired:

> Ain't doin' bad doin' nothin', just settin' round all day. I'm tellin' you the less I do, the more things come my way. When I get up in the mornin', thinkin' o' the day ahead makes me so downright weary, I go right back to my bed. Why should I ever worry? It's such a losin' game! Why should I move when I can prove I get there just the same?

The booze and cigarettes finally caught up with Venuti. He succumbed to lung cancer on 14 August 1978.

45. "FATS" WALLER (1904-43)

Louis Armstrong originated the jazz trumpet, Johnny Dodds the clarinet, Sidney Bechet the soprano sax, and Coleman Hawkins the tenor. What about the piano? Earl Hines was a pioneer, as were James P Johnson, Willie "the Lion" Smith, and most famously "Fats" Waller. They played in a style known as Harlem stride. It was characterised by a strong left hand providing rhythm while the right improvised.

"Rent parties", staged by those down on their luck to pay the landlord, were an important influence on the style. A well-known pianist was hired and admission charged. The party often went all night. The "tickler", as the pianist was known, had to be able to play loud enough to be heard over the noise of the revellers and provide a strong rhythm for dancing. The best of the ticklers, like James P Johnson, were celebrities. They often engaged in "cutting competitions" at jazz clubs with their rivals.

Thomas Patrick Waller was born on 21 May 1904, one of 11 children. His father was a pastor and his mother a musician. Combining the sacred and the profane, young Tom played organ in his father's church and at a local theatre. He benefitted greatly from a close musical and personal relationship with James P Johnson, and by the time he was 15 was a professional musician. Waller is captured at his purest and best in his early solo piano recordings such as "Handful of Keys", "Numb Fumbling", "I've Got the Feeling I'm Falling", "Turn on the Heat", and "Clothes Line Ballet".

A prolific composer, Waller wrote many familiar jazz standards: "Squeeze Me", "Honeysuckle Rose", "Jitterbug Waltz", "I'm Crazy 'Bout My Baby", "Ain't Misbehavin'", and "The Joint is Jumpin'". He is said to have signed away the rights to songs for a plate of hamburgers or a bottle of whisky.

"Fats" complemented his playing with an ability to clown around that was guaranteed to make an audience smile and a uniquely expressive voice – jazz critic and poet Philip Larkin has described it as "an elastic band that can be snapped around any tune" (*All What Jazz*, Faber, 1990). In 1934, Waller began to record with a sextet, Fats Waller and His Rhythm. Tenor player Gene Sedric and trumpeter Herman Autrey were compatible players who provided workmanlike solos and the rhythm section laid down a sturdy swing. With their irrepressible bounce and zest, these records sold extremely well, making Waller rich and a star. The drawback was that Fats was so good at making something out of an inferior tune that he was often given poor material to record. Pressure from his record company to keep producing hits sometimes resulted in superficiality and sloppiness. This has led to critical disapproval. Larkin, for example, has said that in Waller's more routine performances "his humour could be excruciating and his piano-playing a baroque triviality … Both phrasing and facetiousness tremble on the edge of one big cliché" (*All What Jazz*, Faber, 1990).

Even the hard-drinking, happy-go-lucky Waller worried about becoming typecast in his later years:

> Wriggling his eyebrows and scalp, tearing sentimental songs apart, keeping up a constant barrage of quips and cheeky insinuations, he became one of America's most popular entertainers, his musicianship more or less an appendage to his personality. Even the most insensitive of men – and Waller was far from that – would have experienced some sense of frustration in those circumstances (Charles Fox in M Harrison, C Fox and E Thacker, *The Essential Jazz Records: ragtime to swing*, Da Capo, 1988).

The case for the defence is the series of recordings Waller made in London in 1938-39. Fats had a life-long love of the organ and finding one in EMI's famous Abbey Road studio recorded intense, sensitive versions of four spirituals, plus "Lonesome Road" and "Water Boy". He enjoyed playing Bach and in 1938, on a visit to Paris, played the organ of Notre Dame Cathedral – the organist was a fan.

Even more impressive is the *London Suite*, six miniature piano portraits of various parts of the city recorded on 13 June 1939. There are touches of stride and the blues, but it is basically an evocative tone poem, by turns movingly melodic, wistfully reminiscent, and delicately lilting. The musical – if not acoustic – quality is astonishing, especially given the circumstances in which the Suite was composed and recorded. Waller's friend and manager John Kirkeby recalled that Fats had had a particularly heavy night:

> I could see it wasn't the day for his fastest fingering. 'How about working on those pieces you wanted to write about London?' I suggested. I gave him a rapid word picture of Piccadilly, Bond Street, Chelsea, Whitechapel and so on. In three minutes he'd rounded off 'Piccadilly'. And will you believe me when I tell you that those six pieces in the Suite – all original conceptions – were composed and recorded within the hour? What a musician! And Tom was a great guy, too. His heart was as big as the grand piano he played.

Hard living and heavy drinking took their toll – Fats started the day with a shot of whisky he described as his "liquid ham and eggs". He died of pneumonia on 15 December 1943, aged 39. It is fascinating, if saddening, to speculate about what would have resulted if Waller had survived into the 1950s and, like Art Tatum, been sat down behind a good piano with the tape rolling and told to just play.

46. BEN WEBSTER (1909-73)

The holy trinity of Swing-era tenor saxophone players is Coleman Hawkins, Lester Young and Ben Webster. Although in the Hawkins mould, Ben was very much his own man. Webster's style was shadows and light: he contrasted silky threads of melody with thundering, growling passages.

Benjamin Francis Webster was born in Kansas City on 27 March 1909. As a child, he played violin, piano, alto sax, then tenor. Webster quickly established himself in the jazz world, working with major band leaders such as "Cab" Calloway, Benny Carter, Fletcher Henderson and Benny Moten.

With his inimitable taste in musicians, "Duke" Ellington recruited Webster in 1940. He quickly became a key soloist in arguably

Duke's greatest band. Ben was featured on fast numbers such as "Cotton Tail", where he plays with the aggressiveness of a buzz saw, and dreamy ballads like "Chelsea Bridge". The notoriously temperamental Webster left the band in 1943 after heated arguments with Ellington. As a parting gesture, he slashed one of Duke's best coats.

According to Whitney Balliett, Webster had an "enormous lyrical sound and swinging directness – an easy, embracing quality – that touched you in a way that Hawkins and Young, for all their genius, rarely did". He seemed to "breathe rather than play his slow ballads; he'd start phrases with a whispering breath that would grow majestically into a full tone, then gradually melt back into breath— a kind of aural appearing-and-disappearing act". Things tautened when Ben played the blues: "The breathiness vanished, and his phrases became short and hard; he preached and badgered. His ballads insinuated, but his slow blues were in your face" (*New Yorker*, 13 August 2001).

By the 1950s, Webster's style had matured into the epitome of soulful sophistication. This was Ben's golden era. Signing with Norman Granz's Verve label, he made one great record after another. With Verve's house pianist, Oscar Peterson, he cut *King of the Tenors* (1953), *Soulville* (1957) and *Meets Oscar Peterson* (1959). Webster made an LP with Coleman Hawkins in 1957 and two years later recorded *Ben Webster and Associates* with Hawkins, tenor player "Budd" Johnston, and Roy Eldridge on trumpet. There are also two rewarding Verve compilation CDs, *The Soul of Ben Webster* and *Music for Loving*, the latter a "with strings" album that is a cut above the usual syrupy offerings in this genre.

Webster worked prolifically as a sideman with mainstreamers such as altoist Johnny Hodges and trumpeter Harry "Sweets" Edison. One of the best (though least known) of these dates was in

1957 with long-time "Woody" Herman trombonist, Bill Harris. Harris' idiosyncratic yet romantic sound inspired Ben to some of his finest late playing. An unlikely, but successful, combination was a 1959 date with Gerry Mulligan and a west coast rhythm section.

In 1964, Webster permanently relocated to Copenhagen. By now he was in decline due to his alcoholism. Ben was a nasty drunk, nicknamed "the Brute" because of his aggressive behaviour when intoxicated. He recorded regularly but the inspiration had gone out of his playing. The familiar bass rasp had become a cliché and passages that would once have been airy now sounded attenuated.

Ben Webster died of a stroke on 20 September 1973 in Amsterdam. "Ol' Betsy", the saxophone he bought in 1938 and played for the rest of his life, is now part of the collection of the Institute of Jazz Studies at Rutgers. He left specific instructions that it was never to be played again.

47. LESTER YOUNG (1909-1959)

The Swing era was notable for an abundance of outstanding tenor saxophone players, notably Coleman Hawkins, who invented the tenor as a jazz instrument, and his main stylistic rival, Lester Young.

Lester created an entirely new way of playing, which remains influential to this day. He combined compelling legato lines with exciting staccato phrases. The agility and ingenuity of Young's solos is still astonishing. While most tenors growled, he had a light, floating sound with just a touch of asperity. When a fellow tenor player criticised Young for having an alto-like sound, Lester tapped his forehead and retorted: "There's things goin' on up there, man. Some of you guys are all belly".

Musicians as diverse as Charlie Parker and Stan Getz have cited him as an influence. There was a special quality about Lester's playing that attracted adulation. Bop trombonist JJ Johnson recalled: "My first jazz hero ever, jazz improviser hero, was Lester Young. I was a big 'Lester Young-oholic', and all of my buddies were Lester Young-oholics. We'd get together and dissect, analyse, discuss, and listen to Lester Young's solos for hours and hours and hours. He was our god".

Lester Willis Young was born in Mississippi on 27 August 1909 and spent his early years in New Orleans. He saw a lot of America as a young man as part of his father's travelling family band. He played trumpet, violin, drums and alto saxophone before finally settling on tenor sax.

In the early 1930s, Lester moved to Kansas City and soon joined its most famous band, that of "Count" Basie. Quickly realising he had discovered a major talent, Basie featured him prominently. In his early years, Lester had been influenced by "Bix" Beiderbecke's close collaborator, Frankie Trumbauer, who played the light-toned C-melody sax. Exposure to KC jazz added a swinging, bluesy element to his playing.

Lester's first recording session was organised by well-known producer and promoter John Hammond in 1936 with a Basie small group, called Jones-Smith Inc for copyright reasons. His debut was a transformative moment for jazz, like the early work of Louis Armstrong and Charlie Parker. British critic Dave Gelly has said of the session:

> This was the moment when Lester Young finally sidled out of the shadows, the moment when he ceased to be just a name, a rumour from the territory, a set of tall tales con-

cerning jam sessions in bars and hotel lobbies and shoeshine parlours, and became a sound. For the first time, his music was caught, frozen onto shellac grooves and sent out into the world. Forty-five years later, after a lifetime in the record business, Hammond could still categorically say of those three hours, 'It's the only perfect, completely perfect recording session I've ever had anything to do with' (*Being Prez: the life and music of Lester Young*, OUP, 2007).

Young's most productive years were with Basie. The Basie band was one of the greatest of the Swing era with a propulsive drive that would make skeletons jive. Young's solos added a unique brilliance: "Lester Leaps In" and "Jumpin' at the Woodside" are classic examples. Lester also made notable recordings with small groups of Basie-ites in 1938 and 1944. On a session in December 1943 under the leadership of Basie trombonist Dickie Wells, Young recorded some near perfect solos.

Lester was a sympathetic accompanist on many of Billie Holiday's famous late 1930s and early 1940s recordings. They were close friends and Lester coined her enduring nickname, "Lady Day". She responded by christening him "Pres", short for President.

Lester was drafted in September 1944. Army service was traumatic for a sensitive eccentric like Young. He spent most of his time in the detention barracks and was dishonourably discharged in 1945. Lester resumed his jazz career, but much of the inspiration had gone out of his playing. He made recordings for the Aladdin and Savoy labels that sound leaden compared to his former work, although there were moments of creativity. A 1946 date with Nat "King" Cole and "Buddy" Rich elicited some of the old inventiveness.

In the 1950s, Lester signed with Norman Granz's Verve label. Recording for Granz was a kind of pension plan for superannuated musicians. They are sad, almost pathetic records, with Lester sounding like a cliched caricature of his former self, a "hollow crippled voice surrounded by sympathetic but bewildered contemporaries, gamely trying either to hold him up or to cover him up with their own playing" (*Penguin Guide to Jazz*, 6th ed).

Young had a life-long dependence on drugs and alcohol. In his final years he ate little and drank heavily. Lester died on 15 March 1959 at the age of 49.

48. "ZOOT" SIMS (1925-85)

I have to admit to some slight alphabetical sleight of hand to give me a Z. However, it seems appropriate to conclude this book with a musician who, every time I hear him, reminds me of all the things that I liked about jazz in the first place.

"Zoot" Sims had it all: the ability to improvise endlessly; rhythmic ingenuity; effortless swing; a beguiling tone. Influenced by Lester Young, his music was airy, amiable, and infectiously foot-tapping. Whitney Balliett described Zoot as having "a rustic air. His face was rough and handsome and wind-carved. But Sims' exterior was deceptive. It hid a big-city wit who was never off balance, and it hid a player of high lyricism" (*New Yorker*, 12 May 1986).

John Haley Sims was born in California on 29 October 1925. His parents were vaudeville performers and he showed an aptitude for music in his early years, playing clarinet at ten, then switching to tenor saxophone. Zoot left high school early and began working as a professional musician at age 17. He first came to prominence in "Woody" Herman's late 1940s band, which had a famous saxophone section known as "the four brothers": Zoot, Stan Getz, Herbie Steward and Serge Chaloff. Zoot was less ethereal and more propulsive than Stan. He subsequently worked with other top band leaders: Benny Goodman, Stan Kenton, "Buddy" Rich, and Artie Shaw. Sims was also a member of Gerry Mulligan's mid-1950s sextet. He soon graduated to recording as a leader and for the rest of his career mainly worked with small groups. Immaculate, hard-swinging early LPs are the aptly named *Whooeeee* (1956), *Zoot* (1956), and *Down Home* (1960).

Zoot often worked with fellow tenor saxophonist Al Cohn, who replaced Steward in the Herman band. They had a similar style, sound and facility, though Al's tone was gruffer. A typical Sims and Cohn track featured perfectly in tune unison passages, cooking solos, and seamless interweaving as the two split the rideout choruses. They are at their best on *Al and Zoot* from 1957, which features a rare outing from both on clarinet, "Two Funky People". Cohn recalled that "playing was both an escape and a serious vocation for Zoot. He used to talk about the ecstasy factor – the times when your playing becomes a kind of ecstasy" (*New Yorker*, 12 May 1986).

In the 1970s, Zoot, like Ben Webster in later life, specialised in expressive ballad-playing. Hank O'Neal of Chiaroscuro Records arranged recording dates for Sims with Joe Venuti and Dave McKenna. The latter session yielded entrancing versions of "Wherever There's Love" and "I Cover the Waterfront", as well as a swinging

"There'll be Some Changes Made" featuring Sims on soprano sax, an intractable instrument he took up in later life and quickly mastered.

Zoot did his best later work for Norman Granz's Pablo label. The *Penguin Guide to Jazz* (6th ed) has perceptively commented: "Sims could have spent his final years as a nebulous figure. But his Pablo albums set the seal on his stature, sympathetically produced, thoughtfully programmed and with enough challenge to prod Zoot into his best form". Granz recorded Sims with compatible and stimulating partners such as Oscar Peterson, "Count" Basie, Joe Pass and, particularly, Jimmy Rowles. Late masterpieces are: *And the Gershwin Brothers, Soprano Sax, If I'm Lucky, Warm Tenor, I Wish I Were Twins*, and *Blues for Two*. Zoot breezes through his solos with a soft, breathy tone, his consummate musical intelligence still evident.

By the mid-1970s, Sims' alcoholism had reached a chronic stage. He dried out but was claimed by cancer on 23 March 1985. A decade later, Scott Hamilton, a new tenor star much influenced by Sims, and guitarist "Bucky" Pizzarelli, one of Zoot's favourite accompanists, teamed up to make a tribute album, *The Red Door*. Such exercises are often an attempt to cash in on the reputation of the deceased. Not this one – the obvious regard both have for Zoot and his music suffuses the album: swinging, sensitive, sublime. Zoot must have been tapping his foot up in heaven.